COUN

DISCOVERING

GREEN LANES

DISCOVERING GREEN LANES

Valerie Belsey

You road I enter upon and look around, I believe
you are not all that is here
I believe that much unseen is also here.

Walt Whitman, *Song of the Open Road*

GREEN BOOKS
Totnes, Devon

First published in 2001 by
Green Books Ltd
Foxhole, Dartington
Totnes, Devon TQ9 6EB, UK
greenbooks@gn.apc.org
www.greenbooks.co.uk

Additional educational material (suitable for primary
school children) can be found on our website at
www.greenbooks.co.uk/greenlanes.htm

© 2001 Valerie Belsey

Wildlife illustrations by Susan Davies
© 2001 Susan Davies

Cover design by Rick Lawrence

Printed by J.W. Arrowsmith Ltd
Bristol, UK

A catalogue record for this book
is available from The British Library

ISBN 1 870098 96 X

CONTENTS

ACKNOWLEDGEMENTS

I would like to thank my colleagues in both the South Hams District Council and Devon County Council, who provided their expertise so readily; various associations involved in the use of green lanes, who presented their cases fully and fairly; my family and friends; and the many individuals who wrote to me with invaluable information after the publication of *The Green Lanes of England*. These include Omer Roucoux from Dunstable; Victoria Beacon from The British Horse Society; Jenny Dillon from The British Driving Society; Brian Smith from The Long Distance Walkers Association; Tim Allen from North Lincs Environment Team; David Bradbury from The Woodland Trust; Rob Bowker from BTCV; and Jenny Saddington from SOLVE (Save Our Local Valley Environment) in north Somerset. Last but not least, this book would not have been such fun to produce without the genial atmosphere provided by Green Books of Dartington.

INTRODUCTION

Twenty-four storeys up on 94th Street with First Avenue, a dragonfly, then a bee, a pigeon and a few sparrows stream past the window. They fly along the back of the buildings, placed so squarely on New York's grid pattern.

Who knows for how many seasons, how many years, how many centuries they have been using these flight paths, these lanes etched in the sky? Yet now we have forced a lot of creatures into new paths—not least of all our own species. And so it goes on.

Many green lanes of England have until now stuck to their course. This new book is a guide to discovering them in the landscape, on maps and in record offices. It helps you find out who once used them, and who uses them now; the organizations involved in their maintenance, and how to get involved in using and preserving them yourself.

It shows you how wildlife thrives in these cross-habitat corridors. However, owing to the nature of human activities, and the many individual and collective lanes we tread, it is now up to us as individuals to shape the future of our green lanes. We must hope that they won't share the fate of those green tracks which once criss-crossed Manhattan.

New York
October 2000

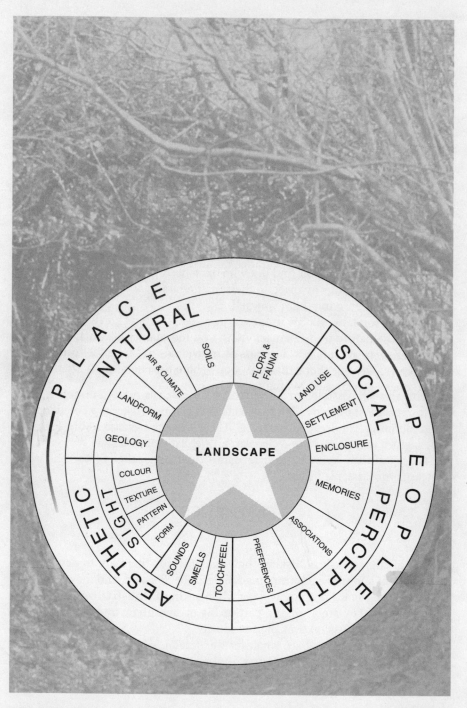

The diagram is taken from the document 'Interim Landscape Character Assessment Guidance', prepared on behalf of The Countryside Agency and Scottish Natural Heritage by Land Use Consultants and Department of Landscape, University of Sheffield, August 1999.

Chapter One

WHAT IS A GREEN LANE?

"A green lane is best defined in broad general terms, viz. that it is an unmetalled track which may or may not be a right of way for the public either on foot, horse, bicycle or motor vehicle, including a motor bicycle, and which is usually bounded by hedges, walls or ditches." (The Countryside Commission, 1979)

Let us define a 'green lane' in terms of separation, and then conjunction: 'green' (meaning green in appearance because of a preponderance of foliage), and 'lane' (meaning a thoroughfare which is often not wide enough for four-wheeled vehicles to pass without one giving way, and which runs between hedges, fences or ditches). Put the two definitions together and you get:

A thoroughfare which is not wide enough for two four-wheeled vehicles to pass without one giving way, which runs between hedges, fences or ditches, and which is green because of a preponderance of foliage.

As with all such Aristotelian definitions, many aspects remain undefined. The chart opposite shows you all the aspects that planners take into consideration when defining 'Landscape Character'. These aspects are all relevant for green lanes, given that many have a circular, tunnel-like appearance.

Let's start with their aesthetic appearance, which is, after all, the one which concerns most people initially.

AESTHETICS

Colour
Green, of course! Ask an Eskimo how many words there are to describe the whiteness of snow, or a desert nomad to describe the sand, and the answer will be just as long as the one you will get when asking a British citizen to describe a green lane: they are a unique part of his or her 'green and pleasant land'. There will be discussion over their verdurity.

But the main fact is that, whatever the season, you will always find some greenness within them, to be found on their surfaces and in their hedgerows and flora.

Form
This is really a question: "When is a lane not a lane?" The answer is: "When it's a green one." The form that green lanes take is determined by the defini-

tion given at the beginning of this chapter, the hedgerows and unmade surface being the most consistent components.

As you will also see from the chart below, the place of the green lane in the highway hierarchy is on the baseline. This brings me to the whole problem of looking at transport systems in terms of hierarchy at all. Engineers use the words 'infrastructure' and 'network', realizing the interconnectedness of all forms of land transport. We, too, use most of them, according to the mode of transport we are using at the time. There is more congestion on the roads than ever before, and opening up green lanes, which are unsuitable for such traffic, will not solve the problem. Green lanes are suffering from so-called 'social exclusion' (just as car-less human beings are said to do). Green lanes were once greatly used and well integrated, but now with changes in legislation they are either to be used by non-motorized forms of transport, or motorized forms—and it is here that the problem of status begins. However, all is not lost, as we will see later when we examine green lane users today.

Pattern

Banking down from out of the clouds and turning towards the mist-clad islands of Britain, the pattern of fields and their hedgerows confirms that we will soon be landing in a climate which does its best to be damper and colder

THE HIGHWAY HIERARCHY SIMPLIFIED

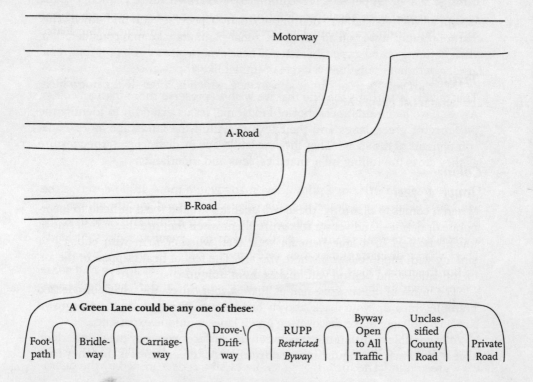

Motorway

A-Road

B-Road

A Green Lane could be any one of these:

| Foot-path | Bridle-way | Carriage-way | Drove-\Drift-way | RUPP *Restricted Byway* | Byway Open to All Traffic | Unclas-sified County Road | Private Road |

than the one we have just left. Although from such great heights we cannot tell whether or not the hedgerows we see flank a green lane, we can sometimes see that they are following a contour line, a watershed, a ridgeway; that they border a series of fields, snake into and out of a settlement, a village or town. The British Isles parcelled up beneath us look very neat and even, though the 'string' of the hedgerows is sometimes broken in places. We know that at ground level, the broken sections are often patched together with fencing and stone walling. Green lanes can often help tie the landscape together again.

How they do this varies enormously within the landscape. Wherever we examine the pattern we are, of course, examining archæological land forms similar to the Reeves on Dartmoor, which reflect ancient communication or trade patterns. They may appear to us to be disjointed, but some were once at the top of the highway hierarchy. A characteristic of green lanes is that they are often to be found in groups; Chapter 3, entitled 'Every Lane has its History', will reveal the reasons why.

If you find an isolated lane, there is every chance that it runs parallel to one of today's heavily used routes, and that it was once a heavily used route itself which has now been left behind by more car-friendly highways (for example several stretches of The Icknield Way and The Ridgeway).

Another characteristic of green lanes is their appearance at a tarmacked crossroads, which often confuses road users: at its beginning, the lane may display some remnant of tarmac. Maybe it is a short cut—but will the under-carriage take it? Or perhaps it is completely overgrown, and a challenge to the rambler armed with secateurs. Finding a green lane *at* a crossroads is one thing—but finding a 'green lane crossroads' is like finding a four-leafed clover.

Texture

This quality is perhaps the one that we wish to preserve more than any other. As we have taken this metaphor of landscape, let us extend it to identify the presence of green lanes and their texture within the landscape as essential components of the scene. They give the landscape its distinct patterned texture as they cross the rolling hills, marshes, fens and moorlands.

Touch & feel

When it comes to planning, these two qualities are the most difficult to incorporate or define—and yet we recognize them when they are there. In terms of touch, the feel of a lane beneath your feet, whether firm with cobbles or sinking with mud, tells you where you are. The feel of heat trapped in the air, or tunnelled wind behind you, makes them unique.

The brush of tall stinging nettles against your calves, the whack of released bramble vines on your back as you bend down to penetrate an overgrown tunnel of foliage, make discovering green lanes a unique experience.

It is possible to differentiate between the surfaces you may meet underfoot. One of the most distinguishing characteristics of green lanes is that they have

The Council for the Protection of Rural England

"On average, traffic on our country lanes may increase by up to 164% over the next 30 years. Bedfordshire, Cleveland, Cambridgeshire, Dorset, Nottinghamshire, East and West Sussex could see threefold increases." (CPRE, 1994)

The CPRE have also made a survey of 'Tranquil Areas' in England. Many green lanes are likely to fall into this category. Here is their definition:

A tranquil area lies:
4 km from the largest power stations.
3 km from the most highly trafficked roads such as the M1/M6; from large towns the size of Leicester and larger); and from major industrial areas.
2 km from most other motor ways and major trunk roads such as the M4 and A1 and from the edge of smaller towns.
1 km from medium disturbance roads i.e. roads which are difficult to cross in peak hours (taken to be roughly equivalent to greater than 10,000 vehicles per day) and some main line railways.
A tranquil area also lies beyond military and civil airfield/airport noise lozenges as defined by published noise data (where available) and beyond very extensive open cast mining.
These areas are draw with a minimum radius of 1 km.

From this it can be seen that the further away from human beings a tranquil area is, the more likely it is that natural sounds will be heard.

untarmacked, unsealed surfaces. These surfaces vary from the clay soils with poor drainage, to be found from the South-East to Oxfordshire and up to the Lake District, to the chalk soils of Kent and Sussex. But even within counties the surface of a lane will vary: for example, in some parts of the Lake District you will find soft peaty soil which is subject to rutting and waterlogging.

The amount of actual 'greenness' in a lane (i.e. vegetation) will affect how it looks, how it is used and how it is maintained. Waterlogging and rutting on a lane is increased when the sun and wind cannot reach the surface because of excessive growth of vegetation.

When working on green lanes, the Department of Environment, Transport and the Regions (DETR) divides sub-base soils into three classes:

Good	gravels, sandy gravels, chalk and rock
Medium	sandy clays and sands, come hard dry clays
Poor	peat, clays, silts and silty clays

More information on how to get closer to the touch and feel of green lanes is given in Chapter 6.

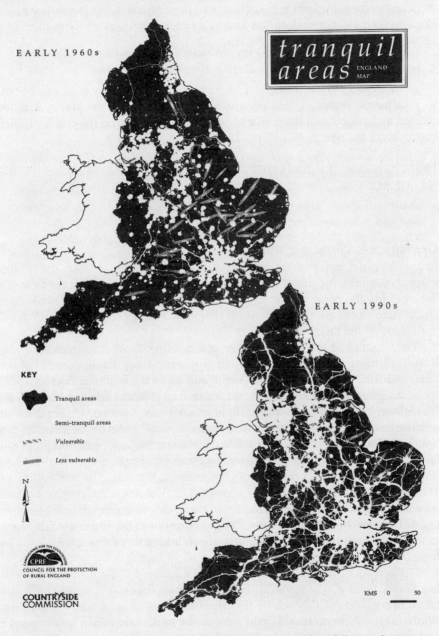

EARLY 1960s

tranquil
areas ENGLAND
MAP

EARLY 1990s

KEY

Tranquil areas

Semi-tranquil areas

Vulnerable

Less vulnerable

N

CPRE
COUNCIL FOR THE PROTECTION
OF RURAL ENGLAND

COUNTRY/SIDE
COMMISSION

KMS   0   50

Green lanes are part of these tranquil areas, both in the countryside and close to the towns.

Smells

In Chapter 4 we will examine in detail the variety of flora and fauna to be found in these wildlife tunnels. They provide a great variety of different smells throughout the year. Suffice to say here that the only unpleasant smells you are likely to find will come from the farmer's muck-spreaders working their way up and down the field behind the lane.

Sounds

What we expect to hear in a green lane, and what we actually hear, can be two very different things. There are the sounds created by people, and those created by indigenous lane-dwellers: bird calls, rainfall, and the rustle of mice and voles in the hedgerows.

This completes the AESTHETICS semi-circle. Let us move on to the NATURAL.

NATURAL

Geology, air, climate & soils

In the centuries before there was heavy road building equipment, the underlying geological structure of the British Isles was a hugely significant factor in determining the route of a road or lane. The forces of limestone, sandstone, chalk, slate shales and granite have all shaped the landscape, and have dictated the course of the lanes.

The varieties of terrain include the glaciated peaks of the North-West, the fertile rolling Midland plateau, the high northern Moors, the low spread of the fens, and the broad sweep of the Downs ending in the white cliffs of Dover.

Many green lanes are sunken, and the reason is primarily a geological one. Man's part in the erosion of the earth is another factor which is more difficult to measure. Sometimes it is clear, as in the case of Telford's building of the South Wales Mail road in Herefordshire, when some adjacent sunken green lanes were robbed of their surface stones for the turnpike.

Landforms

Now we come to another determining factor in defining green lanes: the presence of hedgerows on either side. These can vary in size and materials, such as various combinations of bank, tree, shrub and stone. Once a lane loses its hedgerows, it is in danger of disappearing altogether.

Hedgerows were traditionally used as 'stock dividers', for example separating sheep from cows. Some go back to Roman times, but it was with the farming methods of the Saxons that the parcelling of land really began: the destruction of forests created many hedgerows in its wake. Then between 1750 and 1860 came the Enclosure Acts, when seven million acres of land were enclosed. This sounds like good news as regards hedgerows, but in fact it led to the destruction of many of them as a result of the need to create bigger fields

The Hedgerows Regulations: Your Questions Answered

Do I need permission to remove my hedgerow, either in whole or in part?

YES, if your hedgerow is on, or runs alongside:
- agricultural land;
- common land, including town or village greens;
- land used for forestry or the breeding or keeping of horses, ponies or donkeys; or
- a Local Nature Reserve or Site of Special Scientific Interest.

NO, if it:
- is shorter than 20 metres (unless both ends join up with other hedgerows or
- it is part of a longer hedgerow); or
- is in, or borders, your garden.

Gaps of 20 metres or less are counted as part of the hedgerow. A gap may be a break in the vegetation or it may be filled by, for example, a gate.

You also do NOT need permission to remove your hedgerows:
- to get access—
  either in place of an existing opening, provided that you plant a new stretch of hedgerow to fill the original entrance,
  or when another means of entry is available, except at disproportionate cost;
- to gain temporary entry to help in an emergency;
- to comply with a statutory plant or forestry health order;
- to comply with a statutory notice, for preventing interference with electric lines and apparatus;
- in connection with statutory drainage or flood defence work; or
- to implement a planning permission (but in the case of permitted development rights, most hedgerow removal will require prior permission).

There are further exceptions for reasons of national defence and for removal by the Highways Agency in England or the Secretary of State for Wales as the Highways Agency in Wales.

NORMAL MANAGEMENT OF YOUR HEDGEROW DOES NOT REQUIRE PRIOR PERMISSION.

Extracted from *The Hedgerows Regulations: Your Questions Answered, DOE/Ministry of Agriculture, 1997.* These regulations are still in force.

Sunken Lanes

A frequently asked question is posed here by Leonard Darlington of Ludlow, Shropshire:

"There is one point which I feel that you have not covered sufficiently—the existence of so many sunken lanes, many very deep and many apparently through solid rock. It seems that quite a few were made to reduce the gradient. But when was this done? Is there any historical record? Has there been any research? Some sunken lanes may well be as a result of long use. But, if so, how long?"

As you go through this book you will find the answer to this question appearing in different chapters which relate to the geological position, historical use, maintenance and form of green lanes. One reason for their being sunken is the practice of throwing manure found on the lane base up on to the hedges and trees at the sides. As the hedgerows flourished, the lane sank even more. But the fact that a lane is sunken is not in itself a sign of great antiquity; further evidence must be sought from other sources, as described in the following chapters.

for a growing population. Between 1947 and 1985 about 155,000 kms of hedgerow were destroyed. Recently, however, this trend has been reversed, backed up by the new Hedgerow Regulations of 1995 (see 'Your Questions Answered' on previous page).

In defining the landforms associated with green lanes, we must not discount the fact that many hedgerows have stone beneath their grassy banks, and that many lanes have stone walls as their boundaries, rather than grassy banks.

SOCIAL

Land use, settlement and enclosure

Given the fact that before 1920 all lanes were green, what we see in a green lane is a particular pattern of land use, settlement and enclosure preserved at a certain point in time. It is important that we do not 'fossilize' them, but continue to use them in accordance with the modes of transport for which they were built.

PERCEPTUAL

Memories, associations, preferences

There are many local stories attached to green lanes (not all pleasant), often passed on from generation to generation. These memories can often be kept alive and added to by local information being displayed on illustrated boards or printed trails about the lanes.

Down Memory Lane

Testimonies of a green lane in Dunstable having been used within living memory, which came to light when researching to determine its status: in a case held at the High Court in London over four days in 1891, the following gave evidence:

Richard Riddy, 75, used to drive sheep up it when he was 60 years of age. He came from Aylesbury, along Drover's Way, down this road into Houghton. He also remembers driving up there in a gig and on horseback.

John Cook, 79, of Dunstable had known the road for 65 years, had fetched stone from the quarries along this road for the restoration of Dunstable Church.

Thomas Goodwin, 68, labourer, of Houghton Regis, had known people use the road since he was 6 or 7 years old. Waggons and carts came that way for turf dust. Plenty of carts and waggons used it. Nobody interfered with him. He took timber from Kensworth that way. Should think he went through with timber 40 times, that was 47 years ago.

The prosecution argued that the defendants had been trespassing because it was not a public right of way; or if it was, it was only a footpath. The defendants were acquitted and the road declared to be a public highway. If only present day decisions could be reached so quickly!

* * * * *

We have run round the whole circle of the green lane tunnel in terms of its value in the landscape. It proves its value in every segment.

The definition of a green lane given at the beginning of this chapter is about as accurate as it is possible to get. It is true to say that the whole question of the status of green lanes hinges on arguments about their definition as much as about their appearance. The definition attempts to include all aspects of what it is to walk in a green lane; there are many feelings and reactions which remain undefinable, and change upon revisiting lanes at different seasons and at different times of our life. What are we discovering as we give ourselves up to their greenness? We are entering into the heart of the countryside; when we climb up on their banks we get a very different perspective on the world around us from the one seen by road, sea or air. We cut into ancient landscapes which have changed little since humans started to migrate. Lanes are found in groups—mysterious clusters, sometimes next to towns, to big houses, old industries—or singly, stretching across the landscape and sliding into the shoulders of more major highways.

The next step in discovering them is to fit the definitions to their appearance on maps both ancient and modern.

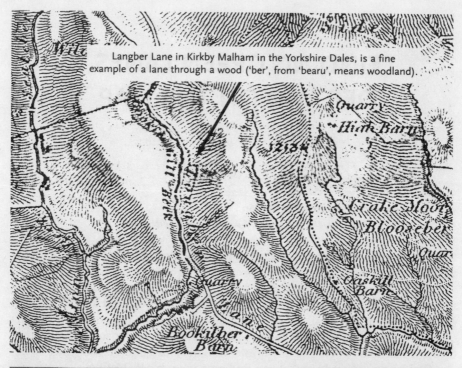

Langber Lane in Kirkby Malham in the Yorkshire Dales, is a fine example of a lane through a wood ('ber', from 'bearu', means woodland).

This is a good example of how useful a map and place name evidence are in dating a lane. The wood you see here was planted in Victorian times, but the lane and woodland site themselves are much older. Mudge's Map may be one of the first records of Langber Lane, and there will further recordings on OS maps and independently produced walking maps of the area. (A colour version of this photograph is in the plate section.)

Chapter Two

FINDING GREEN LANES
OFF AND ON THE MAP

"The son of the athelings, then went over
Steep stone-cliffs, straight passages,
Single tracks, a road untrodden."
—*from Beowulf, the 8th century Anglo-Saxon epic poem*

It is this concept of the road untrodden, the road less travelled, the path not taken which is one of the most attractive aspects of using and researching green lanes.

However, as soon as you wish to know more about them, you will turn to maps and be puzzled by the fact that very rarely will you find a lane actually called Green Lane. And if you do, it could be a complete misnomer in regard to the state that the lane is in today—for example the major road which runs through Palmers Green and down into Woodford in London. Matching what you find on the ground to what you find on a map can be testing.

The simplest and most practical way to do this is to start from a map which is in print today. The main sources of maps are listed below.

Ordnance Survey

At present the new **Ordnance Survey (OS)** 'Explorer' range of maps show unclassified country roads as 'other routes with public access'. They indicate routes that could be green lanes in the following ways:

on the 1:25000 maps, by green dots
on the 1:5000 maps, by magenta dots

If you have traversed on the ground the line shown by green or magenta dots, you will know whether this Right of Way (RoW) is a green lane or not; there is no other way of finding out when using this series of maps. Hedgerows and surfaces are not indicated on them. You will have to go and explore whether or not the lane is bounded by hedgerows and has an unmade surface, in which case it fits the physical definition of a green lane. Some are already signposted with the various Rights of Way signs. If you're lucky, your adventure can go on a little longer, as everybody likes discovering an unsignposted road—it is indeed a discovery. (Refer to Chapter 5, 'Use Them or Lose Them', to find out more about categories of Public Rights of Way).

If you are still checking for the status of the lane, then at this stage it would be advisable to go and look at the **Definitive Map** for your area, which is kept at your local County Hall.

If you are not just checking for status, but are more interested in the historical value of a lane and wish to discover it on other maps, then this is the route you must take: stick with the **Ordnance Survey** maps. First, go in search of earlier editions either in your local library (in the Parish Boxes), Records Office or second-hand book shop, a Solicitor's Office, Estate Agent's Office, the Council Planning Office, the Highways Authority or the local Museum. When searching for these, you must choose your time to visit diplomatically. From my experience, it's true to say that the welcome you receive in these places will depend as much on the way the wind is blowing as on your attitude. You should remember that the fate of a footpath may be of importance to your village, but the maps on which it appears might also be needed urgently to sort out the location of broken culverts on a flood plain.

Once you have located the maps, these are some of the editions where your green lane may appear as a Right of Way (ROW), track or white road:

- The very early editions, known as **Mudge's One Inch Maps** (circa 1800).
- The early **OS two and a half inch maps** in your area are a good place to start when searching for green lanes, as are the **6" OS maps**, dating from the 1870s, which are always available in Records Offices.
- On the **OS 6" maps 1:10, 560 series**, first produced in 1889, you will find all tracks and paths recorded as well as early Ecclesiastical and Civil boundaries.
- After this there is the **First Series of the 1:150,000** sheets.

Remember that some green lanes are boundary lanes, and that boundaries do not appear on modern 1:50,000 ('Landranger') maps. The **1:25,000 ('Pathfinder') maps** are useful for green lane tracking.

What is a Definitive Map?

"Definitive maps are legal record of the public's rights of way. Local authorities are responsible for them. If a right of way is shown on the map, that is conclusive evidence, in law, that the public have those rights—and still have them unless there has been a legally authorized change.

Definitive maps are a major element in providing evidence of the existence of public rights of way but they may not show the full picture. There may be additional rights over the land which have not yet been recorded on the map, or they may be rights which are incorrectly recorded on the map. For example, if a way is shown on the definitive map as a bridle way it is conclusive evidence that there are rights of passage on foot, horseback and bicycle but there may also be vehicular rights which have not been recorded on the map. Maps can be amended if evidence of missing rights of way is discovered, or there is a need to correct errors in previously recorded information."

(The Countryside Commission, 1998)

Tithe maps (circa 1840)

Because of their scale, these maps can be very useful in identifying every twist and turn in a green lane. It is not only the map which will be of interest, but also the Apportionment which goes with the map, in which the owner, tenant and perhaps the name of the lane but certainly the adjacent field names are listed, and sometimes the names of highways, all cross-referenced by numbers and letters on the map. You will find these maps in your local Records Office, and there should also be a copy in your Parish Chest—or maybe the Vicar has it for safe keeping.

By working backwards from present-day maps, you will see how quickly we slip into another age of transport. You will be looking at maps which were made in an age before motorized vehicles.

These maps are physically great fun to research, as their size makes them very unwieldy. You will be provided with some hefty weights to stop them curling up as you move from one section to another.

Also belonging to these early years is the sale of Estate Papers which may be lodged in the vaults of a local Solicitor or Estate Agent. Before the horse-drawn carriage slips over the hill for ever, it is also a good idea to consult any Estate papers which may be in existence. These could be lodged with the Records Office or still be part of the Estate. Tracks, Rights of Way and Carriage Runs may all appear on any remaining maps.

Turnpike routes

You will find these in Records Offices in the Highways Section of the County Council's Records. All sorts of papers relating to the Turnpike can be found, and you might be lucky enough to find a map too. Once again, a local Solicitor or Estate Agent may have copies he does not know about in his vaults, as Turnpike Trusts were managed by groups of local businessmen and set up for their profit and convenience.

Highways Boards

The Highways Boards which were set up in 1835 often produced maps which were used in the contemporaneous Church Survey for the gathering of Tithes. A Records Office or the Planning Department of a County Council may still be in possession of maps relating to these new areas of legislation.

Parish records

The Parish Record Books which you will find in Records Offices are worth scouring for contents, which may include an old map or two. You will find these by consulting the Parish Registers files and then noting down the number of the document you require.

Amenities

The founding of Water Boards, Railway, Tram and Bus Companies in the nineteenth century led to the production of maps, which in some cases still exist in

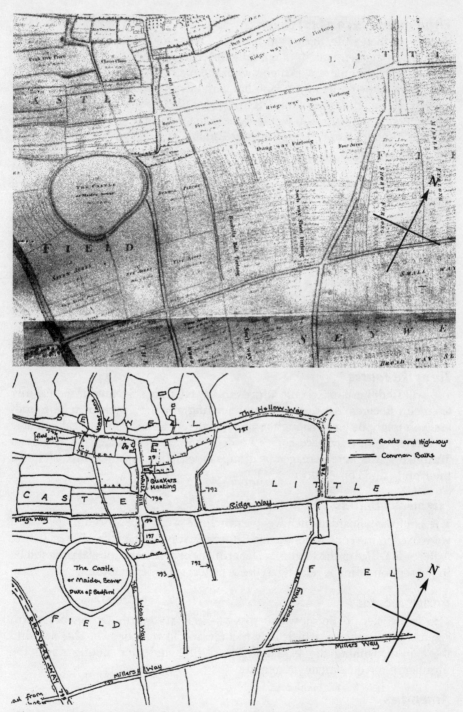

The top map shows the north section of the Duke of Bedford's estate in 1762, and the one below is captioned as follows: "Containing the manors of Houghton Regis and Seywell, belonging to John Duke of Bedford, surveyed by T. Bateman in 1762, copied by T. Richardson in 1766."

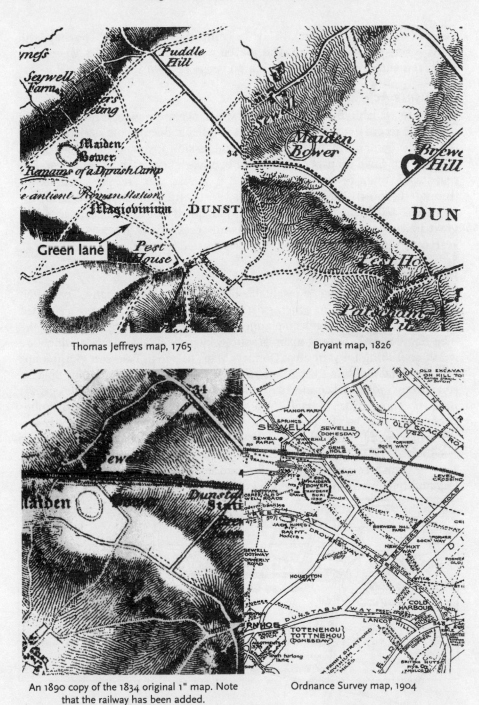

Thomas Jeffreys map, 1765

Bryant map, 1826

An 1890 copy of the 1834 original 1" map. Note that the railway has been added.

Ordnance Survey map, 1904

This group of green lanes around Totternhoe, near Dunstable, will be found at the following OS grid reference: TL008214. Use Maiden Bower as a reference point for finding today's green lane.

Records Offices or in the archives of the companies themselves. The maps will show where the vehicles ran, and maybe where projected routes were to be built, sometimes along green lanes at the edge of towns.

Enclosure Acts

These are available from the 1700s onwards. We are now entering the world of private records, rather than those more reliable documents associated with the public domain. Map-making was a profession invented by the gentry in order to put down on paper where their boundaries were, so all could see. The maps could often be very detailed, down to the last tree and the last trackway through the forest. These records can be very useful in dating a lane, as important trees and hedgerows were not only mapped but described in detail. A great pollarded oak or a coppice plot with access via a green lane is worth searching for.

Individual surveyors' accounts

Sometimes these can be an invaluable help in dating a green lane. They often show not only the roads which existed but also those which were projected (some of which may have been planned to be turnpikes). Here are some of the most famous early County maps produced by individual surveyors, which are worth consulting for your area: Donne's Maps (c. 1765), Paterson's strip maps (c. 1784), and Ogilby's Strip Maps 1600-1676 (*Britannia* 1675); John Speed's (1552-1629) individual county maps found in *The Theatre of the Empire of Great Britain*; John Norden's (1548-1626) *Speculum Britanniæ*; and Christopher Greenwood's series of 1" to the mile maps (circa 1820). Find out which surveyor first operated in your area. The maps are usually available on a scale of one inch to one mile.

The Ordnance Survey have also produced a map of Seventeenth Century England (published in 1930) which is useful for this period.

This early OS legend (1" to 1 mile map from 1921) shows what might turn out to be green lanes on the ground today. Only those roads 'good and fit for fast traffic' appear in red. Those from 'fit for ordinary traffic' to 'other roads' appear in orange, and from 'bad' downwards in black and white. 'Bad' roads are usually today's green lanes.

The drovers' routes

You will now need to join the dots together. By this, I mean that it is unlikely that you will find, for example, a map drawn up by a droving company, but the clues which exist along a route will enable you to project the route which the drovers once took (see Chapter 3, 'Every Lane has its History'). If you take a long section of a well-known Drover's Way such as The Kerry Ridgeway or The Long Mynd, you can try to find out just how much of the route was covered by green lanes. For more detailed information, see the Appendix on Drover's Routes in *The Green Lanes of England*.

Trade routes

Some sections of these may still be green lanes—for example, the Cheshire Salters Ways. It appears that no one has matched these known salt routes to the present day Rights of Way network. Undoubtedly, parts will be tarmacked, and some parts not recorded as public Rights of Way. I understand that it may be possible to relate descriptions in the writings about the salters' ways to OS Maps at 1:2500 scale, which give information on public Rights of Way. As far as I know, no one has walked these lanes with the view of discovering whether they are green lanes or not—this is just one area where pioneer work is needed.

Industrial records

Whenever a mine was opened up and mining rights were purchased, maps were involved. Some green lanes once existed as access routes to mines, and many survive in areas which have now been opened up for recreational purposes, such as those to be found leading down to Morwellham Copper Quay in Devon.

Earlier industries from Lincolnshire are evident on the ground in the form of Turbury (peat) paths. What is typical of Turbury lanes is that they all appear to be interrelated, and form small self-contained groups which serve their particular purpose. The present-day grid pattern of roads which can be found in industrial estates on the outskirts of towns and cities is similar in its origin.

The Elizabethans

As we go back in time, the accuracy of available maps declines, but they can show details which still remain today, such as The Queen's Highway in East Allington, Devon. The Queen in question is Elizabeth I, and the green lane still survives in Queen Elizabeth II's day.

Parish records may contain maps relating to the Beating of the Bounds (the once annual ceremony of tracing on the ground the limits of an ecclesiastical parish), although more often than not only a written account remains. It is worth searching the Parish Registers for this evidence.

The mediæval period

The mapmaker John Norden (1548-1626), was appalled by the behaviour of those mediæval landlords who evicted residents in order to obtain their arable land for sheep grazing. There may be Estate records which include maps of these new divisions of land. The famous historian W. H. Hoskins, writing about this period, said:

> "Practically all the thousands of farm names printed on the modern map would have been on the earlier map, could it have been drawn; and nearly all the thousands of miles of lanes and by-roads would have existed also."

In his book *The Roads and Tracks of Britain*, Christopher Taylor goes on to say that the same is probably true of large areas of Cornwall, Wales and the Marches, and much of northern England and Scotland. Yet if these farmsteads and routes were there in the eleventh century, how much earlier might they be?

It is possible to make your own green lanes map showing mediæval lanes in your area, by plotting out all the farm foundation dates and linking them up with the roads which exist today—whether they are still green or not. What you will see is an early pattern of communication, and in some cases lanes which have remained green from mediæval times onwards.

Ecclesiastical records

Before the Dissolution of the Monasteries in 1539, it was the duty of these establishments to maintain roads and bridges. Their records may reveal the presence of green lanes.

All the above maps must be considered alongside other historical evidence relevant to the period, which is set out in the next chapter. A map, a historical document and the lane itself are all proof positive for dating and recording a green lane.

There are four Ordnance Survey specialist maps for this period. The first appeared in 1935 and was called Britain in the Dark Ages: South Sheet (2nd ed. 1966) and in 1938 a sheet for the North followed. There then followed in 1954-55 a sheet for Monastic Britain, and a second edition in 1958.

If there is a green lane close to an ecclesiastical settlement, this is another clue to the lane's age. Working from documents such as Bishop's Visitations and Feet of Fines (described in Chapter 3), it is possible to make your own maps by joining up the Visitation points.

Roman roads

Although we do not have any maps made by the Romans themselves, we do have a lot of maps compiled by those who came after and wished to plot where their roads once led. Besides the sources listed in Chapter 3, you may also wish to consult the following OS publication, which should be available in most Records Offices: the Map of Roman Britain (1st edition 1924, 2nd edition 1931, 3rd edition 1956). Many OS maps around 1900 will refer to an old track as a 'Roman Road', but this is not a complete validation of its date. A good place to start is any edition of Ivan Margary's *Roman Roads*, mentioned in the bibliography. The maps given in this volume cover all regions of the UK, and it includes a very useful guide to discovering Roman roads on the ground—roads which, of course, may not necessarily be green lanes. Apart from

Drovers Lanes in Dunstable

Discovering a group of lanes is always a thrill. Here is a description of the Totternhoe group near Dunstable (maps, including one from the Duke of Bedford's Estate papers, are shown on pages 22 & 23). The group of lanes is surprisingly to be found in a sprawling suburban landscape. When I visited these lanes, having trekked out by bus from Luton to Dunstable and walked along West Street in streams of suburban traffic, the appearance of Drover's Way (tarmacked) at the head of yet another housing estate did not bode well.

I knew that Drover's Way wasn't the real green lane, but beyond the cast iron barrier and the sign showing a byway and the Chilterns Way, the real green lane appeared: a magnificent 40-foot-wide strip of history, running straight through a housing estate, protected by rows of tall beeches and flanked by stringy blackthorns.

The ice-cream van tinkled a traveller's tune; obscured from view by the trees, it sounded as if it were a hunting horn. By the time I reached the first turn to Totternhoe, I was breathing the clean air of Dunstable Downs. Horse-riders, dog-walkers and bikers all use this lane, which seems to have a footpath running along one of its banks and is hidden by foliage for most of its way. A regular user told me that only tractors ever came up here; to his knowledge there were never any cars.

The green lane opens out at the entrance to the prehistoric Maiden Bower over the fields. From there you can look back and enjoy the plummeting performances of the microlites and hang-gliders up on the Downs. Higher up in the sky streak the twentieth century's favourite mode of transport—planes, wafting you from Luton to destinations worldwide. With the increase in motorized traffic in all areas, you can understand why the local residents who regularly use this lane have accepted their classification as 'Byways'. For if the lanes were to be classified as bridleways or as footpaths, they would be under threat of losing their historic width—and the uplifting 'whoosh' of wildness they give to the landscape for those lucky to live close to them.

seeking alignments with those already recorded, there are other relevant clues for identifying Roman roads:

1. An embankment with metalling beneath.
2. Parallel ditches or large hollows which have provided material for the embankment.
3. A distinct cutting where the road descends.
4. Scattered metalling of artificial origin, such as iron slag.
5. Scattered gravel, if not local.
6. Traces of laid stonework, kerbs, cobbles or a foundation layer of stone blocks.

Where Roman roads are now green lanes, they certainly didn't begin as such.

The hedges which are now in place grew up gradually along their length either to disguise their presence or as a result of neglect. A good example of this is the Roman Ridge north of Doncaster (28b) in Margary's map 'South of Woodlands, Doncaster, looking North', which had a high agger now covered by a footpath and high hedges.*

One of the longest green lanes which is a Roman road is Sewestern Lane, which branches off from Ermine Street near Greetham (Margary's no. 580). It carries on right to Sedgebrook.

Of course many Roman roads which are now green lanes are associated with Roman settlements, for example Silchester. Margary writes:

> The Hants-Berks county boundary now follows the line for 2 miles over Riseley Common, most of it along a green lane with traces of an agger, 15 feet wide, along its south side.

Margary warns us against looking for old holloways, especially where the ridge between two adjacent hollows has the rounded profile similar to that of an agger; holloways are usually too steep-sided to fall into the category of Roman road.

The prehistoric periods

Although cave paintings have been discovered which relate to man's early hunting activities, no maps have yet been found showing his early routes across the earth. However, many such maps do exist, having been constructed by historians and archæologists.

I quote from an excellent little series of essays by the highway historian Roger Millington, which appeared in the 'Reflections' column in *3M Magazine* some years ago. With tongue in cheek, he gives

Is The Long Man of Wilmington one of the first map-makers? Are his two poles surveyor's rods?

guidelines (which he calls a 'recipe for a mystery') for those who wish to hunt out 'ley lines' in the landscape:

1. Take a 1" Ordnance Survey Map of the British countryside, avoiding mountainous or built-up areas.
2. Look for earthworks, standing stones, tumuli, barrows, hillforts, mottes and baileys, crosses, stone circles and religious buildings.
3. Draw a small circle round each one that you find.
4. Now take a long clear plastic straight-edged ruler. See how many points you can align along the straight-edge. Where an earthwork covers some area you can align along any of the banks or through a central mound if one is shown. Draw

---

* When an agger is referred to as being evidence of a Roman road remember that it refers to the raised central section of the road and not the ditches and hedges which flank it.

Researching green lanes

Omer Roucoux, from the Dunstable and District Local History Society, writes:

"There is a Green Lane in Dunstable visible on old maps and still existing as a footpath between two rows of very tall trees. If you are interested I could provide you with copies of old maps and of recent ones, I am writing to you now because a public enquiry will be held in Dunstable on 16th February 1998, about the re-classification of it. It is, as I said, presently a footpath (RUPP) blocked by bollards, but for unknown reasons South Bedfordshire County Council have the intention to make it a 'byway opened to all traffic', and the bollards would be removed. Peaceful people who like to walk their dogs there are frightened that it will become a practising place for motorbikes and other abuses,"

Mr. Roucoux advised that there were two and half kilos of paperwork to go with this decision. Maybe these will be recycled one day in a planting scheme for the lane to which they refer. This is an example of the amount of evidence from maps and other sources that you can come across in researching green lanes.

---

a pencil line along the straight-edge only when you find five or more points in alignment.
5. Don't do this in the presence of an archæologist, or you will be labelled as a 'nutcase'.

The alignment of such monuments was first checked by Alfred Watkins (particularly in the Shropshire area), and there are many examples of his maps in his book *The Old Straight Track*. Today his work is continued by Danny Sullivan (see Bibliography).

Apart from making your own maps for this period, here are one or two for reference. Hippisley-Cox's work, *The Green Roads of England*, which contains watershed maps, is worth consulting for prehistoric routes, and Grundy's Ridgeway Maps for ridgeways. The Ordnance Survey have produced several useful maps for the period: Neolithic Wessex (1932); Ancient Britain (1951, 2nd edition 1964); Southern Britain in the Iron Age (1962); Britain Before the Conquest (1974); and the Bodleian Map of Great Britain AD 1360 (known as The Gough Map) is also worth consulting.

MAPPING GREEN LANES TODAY

Useful projects which might be undertaken to record green lanes today include the mapping of any created as a result of the building of major roads such as the M25, or in the future any from the Rail Link Green Plan around the Channel Tunnel development in Kent. In order to check these out, consult the HMSO publication *The Channel Tunnel Rail Link Act* (1996). Chapter 61 of

Schedule 3 of the Act contains the relevant information. With new road schemes constantly appearing, checks need to be made to see how they will cut across existing green lanes—or create them.

Green lanes appearing on title deeds

Should you be lucky enough to buy a property which has a Right of Way running through it, then the procedure for identifying this is given here.

Jonathan Cheal is a solicitor with an extensive farming and landowning practice. Writing in the GLEAM (Green Lanes Environmental Action Movement) Newsletter of Autumn 1998, he outlined the complexities of dealing with the incorrect classification of BOATs and RUPPs (see Chapter 5). I quote below from his advice concerning estate papers. He gives advice about looking at the deeds of a property; even if the tracks are not shown on the deeds, they may have been overlooked and rights over them may still exist.

> "The freehold of such tracks is probably still vested in the trustees of the old estate or their successors. If you don't own the trackway itself but you do own the land both sides of it, then there is a presumption that you own the trackway unless somebody can show a better claim. Check the deeds for grants or reservations of private rights of way (not necessary if the track was public)."

Land registration

Regarding the registration of property or land which contains a right of way (which may or may not be a green lane), Jonathan Cheal advises as follows:

> "There is much misunderstanding here. Compulsory registration now covers the whole of England and Wales, but land which hasn't changed hands for some years is not registrable at HM Land Registry. Now that there is a right to inspect and search the register, some claimants have done so and, finding a track unregistered, have assumed wrongly that it is 'ownerless land', and thus automatically subject to public rights. This is clearly a false assumption; it is always as well to remember the difference between ownership and rights."

Although nothing can replace the thrill of discovering green lanes for yourself, there are now plenty of local guides which will indicate which part of a trail is a green lane. In *The Edward Thomas Country* by W. M. Whiteman, there is an example of one of many trails nationwide which include green lanes in their make-up. Here he is referring to 'The Lane', a poem written by Thomas about a lane in Hampshire:

> "Green Lane, says the poem later, is a mile long and ends suddenly, and it has a glint of hollies in the hedge. The blackberries, harebells and dwarf gorse are still there. the hollies now stand up above the hedge like sentries at intervals. The lane does end suddenly. It is broad because enclosure commissioners always made their new roads to standard widths, with a grass verge on one or both sides."

Besides checking the Ordnance Survey maps, it is possible to discover green lanes on maps produced by other publishers (such as Bartholomews), or the

Extract from Ogilby's Strip
Maps, 1675

early series of Contour Maps for Cyclists. The best advice is not to discount anything, and to keep searching both in libraries and second-hand bookshops.

However many maps you find which give you an indication of the original purpose, location and age of your lane, there is nothing to equal the thrill of discovering them on the ground. This can happen more easily when you are out in the country under your own steam, or at least not under fossil fuel power of any kind. A green lane may suddenly form part of a network of footpaths or bridleways. One may appear in the distance as a gap in the hedge, and you might assume it to be a gateway—but on arrival discover that it is a green lane tempting you forward. Never resist that temptation, however faint the light at the end of the tunnel may be.

Monthly
WEEKLY ACCOUNT of Money expended on the Highways of the

Day of *December* 1835

from the *25th*

DAY LABOR & WHEN PERFORMED.	LABORERS' NAMES.	No. of Days.	Rate per Day.	£.	s.	d.
	R. Clarke	2	20d		6	4
1838.	D.°	4½	16d	1		
Dec. 20, 28,	Geo. Spatleman					
1839.						
Jan. 14, 15, 16, 23;						
Lun. 14 & dam.						

Chapter Three

EVERY LANE HAS ITS HISTORY

"Long ago, before the Phoenicians came to Devon, this old lane was a way for men and horses and cattle; a track which, slowly sinking under the scrape of sleds on the soft grey rock, the peck of pack-horse hooves, and the courses of rain in winter, for centuries has remained the same."—Henry Williamson in *The Lone Swallows* (1930), describing Vention Lane at Putsborough Sands, North Devon.

One of the most contradictory facts about green lanes is that so many which are used for recreation today have their origins in sweated labour. The number of gentlefolk using them for recreational purposes in Jane Austen's day, for example, were few, and the inclement weather and parlous state of the surface would certainly have made them seek out the better maintained highroads. Does this mean that, by a process of inheritance, they naturally belong to today's working classes alone, to the likes of long-distance lorry drivers on their days off?

If this is the case, then the fact that they are principally populated by the marching and galloping middle classes goes a long way to explaining why the wrangles over who can walk when and where sometimes seem to be founded on shifting sands. We must never forget that in the UK we live in a man-made landscape, and that lanes have changed according to their use over the years.

Besides all the acronyms which refer to the legal status of a lane, and also those which represent green lanes user groups, there is one which I have been using for some time which is of relevance when discussing their historical value—GRUTHs (Green Routes Used Throughout History).

Although finding out who used green lanes in the past can be of some help when determining their present and future status, it is also a fascinating pursuit in itself; there is no good reason to believe that Drovers' Ways, Truss Ways (used by harvest waggons) or ways to market towns will be reinstated as a result of your researches!

As with all journeys, a walk down a green lane which has personal memories is one way of keeping it alive and of adding to its history.

WHERE OUR ANCESTORS ONCE TROD

Finding out where our ancestors actually lived and breathed will always have a fascination and can, incidentally, lead to the discovery of a green lane down which your grand-daddy once strolled.

If you wish to find out where your ancestors once worked, try walking around the area where they once lived. It may prompt you to ask who, apart from your forebears, used a particular lane, and why?

Tracing Your Ancestors

Shortly after the publication of *The Green Lanes of England*, a Mr. Andrew Belsey wrote to me from Wales with some interesting comments on the book, but no mention of the fact that his name was the same as my matrimonial one. A reply was sent, and correspondence ensued about the various branches of the Belsey family.

Some of the members of the one into which I married came from the area between Canterbury and Deal. A William Belsey was born in 1809 and lived to the age of 93—a heartening fact to pass on to one's children. William was a footman, valet, dairyman, possibly a publican, and he was born in a village called Ash. He walked along these roads, and more to the point drove his cattle along them. This area of Kent has many references to drovers' roads, such as Potts Farm Drove, Drover's End, Cop Street Drove, and Goldstone Drove (which leads to Minster). So these Belseys were agriculturalists who subsequently went into service. Was this out of necessity, or from connections? The family tree shows that William Belsey's mother was illegitimate, and that she might have been brought up by the Ewell family of Sandwich. Was there some obligation upon this family to provide employment for her children hereafter? If so, this would explain William's various careers, peaking as a publican.

Just before going into Ash church, I went down Pudding Lane (a Bridleway leading to Drover's End) and then up round the footpath along Ship Lane and into the church of St. Nicholas. I posed a question to one of the churchwardens about the persistent presence of the Belseys, and received an instant reply: without batting an eyelid, he replied that one Ian Belsey was his neighbour. 'All roads lead to Rome', is all that I can say!

In Kent, the gentle landscape, divided by lines of poplars, willows and big skies, leads to the coast ahead—and to all sorts of transcontinental traffic. Along the Stour Valley Walk and the Elham Valley Way you will find some green lanes cutting through the greensand, flint and chalk soil. I use this example as an opportunity to think of green lanes' history in personal, as well as document-researching, terms: "Every lane has its history; it is not just there by accident," as the historian Hoskins once said.

Today we are seeing a reverse in the trend of rural to urban migration. Traffic in rural areas is on the increase. Between 1981 and 1997 traffic grew three times faster on rural A roads (by 75%) than on urban roads (by 23%). It seems likely that green lanes will either be destroyed, or be brought into the road system. However, there is some doubt as to whether the current system will continue as it is; we shall just have to wait and see. Patterns of travelling to work could change (and the old mill path could become open for commercial traffic once again). If more buses and trains are scheduled on A and B roads, green lanes might become access routes to these roads.

Green lanes once led to market towns for commercial exchanges, such as those involving corn, sheep and everyday necessities. Nowadays such towns are sometimes the locus for the sales of finished products, services and banking.

Using the historical divisions already established in *The Green Lanes of England*, let us see what source material is available for dating them.

GREEN LANES IN THE PREHISTORIC AND ROMAN PERIODS

The prehistoric landscape was one of discovery. The routes were long, for people were still hunting and gathering as they moved over the land. This gave rise to two kinds of green lane which have evolved as the result of neglect: parts of major routes such as The Icknield Way, and those which existed as feeder lanes to other ridgeways.

Prehistoric man cleared the ground, grazed his cattle and then moved on. It was the landscape of nomads, who worked without maps. But the roads acted as maps on the ground, such as the Cursus at Dorchester-on-Thames, where there are parallel alignments in the form of earthen banks with quarry ditches outside them, built around 3000 BC. There were others that were strongly connected to religious sites.

Lanes which belong to Prehistoric times, although the oldest, can be the least used today. Large sections of the Icknield Way, The Ridgeway, and sections of The Pilgrim's Way, still have surfaces that remain untreated since animals and people first made tracks along them.

Alfred Watkins, in his pioneering book *The Old Straight Track*, set out some practical tips to follow when tracing ley lines which, he suggested, linked pre-

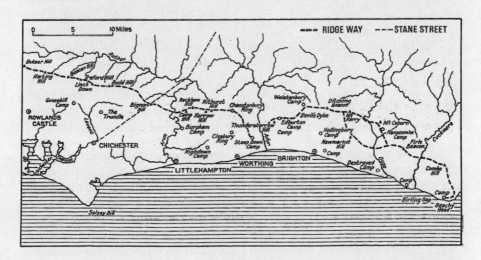

A section of R. Hippisley-Cox's map of the South Downs ridgeway. Many of the camps, rings and beacons shown here are accessible via green lanes.

Evidence on the Ground

Mervyn and Val Benford are involved in recording highway furniture, and I quote from the newsletter for the 'Milestones' organization dated August 2000. It is an example of finding interesting unexpected evidence on the ground.

"We visited a trackway, once the old Coach Road from London to Bath plying an ancient Roman route near Calne, long by-passed by the later A4. Two correspondents knew of it and the old stones still stood. We found one, virtually illegible, but in locating it had asked two people for help who had lived all their lives nearby but they had never seen the stones! One correspondent knew this road went along other relatively unknown tracks and was able to connect it with milestones deeper into Wiltshire of which we did not know. In such examples, one realizes how valuable mile-markers are in preserving the evidence of earlier road networks and travel routes."

historic settlements, burial and religious sites. These are strong clues to tracing them on the ground. (See Chapter 2, 'Green Lanes On and Off the Map'). Some of the tracks which lead to these sites are green lanes.

However it is as well to remember that in Prehistory, people spent most of their time around their homes. The domestication of animals such as sheep and horses is seen between 4000 and 2000 BC, from which time we can begin to trace these patterns of domestication in the landscape.

Drake Lane, which follows the old Jutish trackway across the North Downs just east of Hollingborne, is a good example of this.

The map on page 35 shows the watersheds (i.e. areas of dry land between two wet areas which led down to estuaries and ports). As water transport predates land transport, it is a good idea to look at these kind of routes when looking for prehistoric lanes. Ridgeway maps are available at local levels, such as Grundy's Maps for the South West, Oxfordshire and other areas.

The Jurassic Way was thought to have run from Lincoln to Glastonbury, and therefore any green lanes which run off from this line could be Prehistoric in origin. There are also trade routes, such as those by which chert tools were carried long distances from Cornwall and from Grimes Graves near Thetford.

Examples of the hand axe, for which the best materials came from Cumbria, have been found in many parts of Britain. By joining these sites up it would be possible to build up a network of those parts of the route which still survive as green lanes.

Hillfort terraces have sometimes developed from sunken green lanes which were used as works access routes. You will also find green lanes leading into hillforts and religious sites, and surviving in short stretches around these monuments.

Although one would assume that the green lanes which date back to this early period would be the most sunken, this is often not the case. They were built on exposed areas of ground which were safe, visible and comfortable to travel along.

When they arrived, the Romans would have incorporated the existing road system which they found, leaving them as feeder roads to their new main ones, or in some cases building over them. In the main, they were used to march armies from one administrative centre to another. There are many excellent studies of Roman roads in the UK, and increasing evidence to suggest that what were once thought of as roads dating from previous periods were in fact Roman. However, in Wiltshire Roman roads were ignored as Parish Boundaries, and those set down in the Iron Age are still used. Some Roman roads which were no longer used became colonized with the trees and shrubs which were later cleared back to form hedgerows, thus qualifying them for green lane status. Greenways or green paths are often referred to as Roman roads on early maps, but further evidence must be sought.

BUILDING THE NETWORK OF GREEN LANES IN THE DARK AGES

The invasion of Britain by Anglo-Saxons from mainland Europe took place over a long period of time, and in many cases involved settlement along tried and tested routes. It was primarily a peaceful movement by a people seeking more living space. But what about those Britons who were still here?

Think of those poor desperate travellers who crept out on to our highways after the Romans had gone. They would have been the Celts and Ancient Britons, whose main routeways, such as the Icknield Way, had been taken over. But now they were free to travel as they wished.

The language of the new invaders—the Anglo-Saxons—still remains as evidence of this new course of invasion, with some Celtic remnants appearing, which may be pre- or post-Roman.

The Saxons came seeking land and living space, and yet the word *here*, meaning 'an invading army', appears 221 times in the Anglo-Saxon charters. These charters are a rich source of historical evidence for finding routes still represented by green lanes in the landscape.

One in six of the features mentioned in these early English charters is to do with highways (there are more examples in the Midlands than elsewhere). The charters often refer to *gemære hagan* (boundary hedges). The boundary stones which appear in these charters are referred to as *mærstance*. These stones came to be known in some cases as 'hoarstones', which might be describing their greyness, although *here* refers to invading armies, as we have just seen.

Our parish boundaries were first recorded in the Ancient Parish List, the Papal Taxation Order (*Taxito Ecclesiastica Angliae et Walliae, auctoritate Papae Nicholai IV*, circa 1291) published by the Royal Commission in 1802. If you want to find out the true status of your parish boundary, then this is the document to which you should refer.

Settlement patterns can be traced through place names which have an Anglo-Saxon content. However, where you find large or double hedge bound-

aries flanking parish boundaries, they might be roads which were incorporated into parish boundaries or became them over time, as parishes began to
be sub-divided. Examples of Saxon boundary lanes can be found at:

- Old Hundred Lane in Suffolk between Bosmere and Hartismere
- In Middlesex at Grimsdyke between Pinner Green and Harrow Weald
Common
- In Wiltshire at Witherington Down towards the village of Redlynch (a
track dates back to 843)

In Northamptonshire, part of Watling Street in the Crick area was once an
Anglo-Saxon land boundary. Parish boundaries began as ecclesiastical divisions of land, and were bounded by the church where you were baptised and
buried. The civil boundaries are different: they refer to the official body to
whom you pay taxes and rates. In general, the 'vill' was the basic unit of local
administration, to which royal courts and tax collectors worked: this unit, not
the manor, was used for collecting money. The vill of the thirteenth century is
the 'civil parish' of the 19th. It was from these divisions that the royal court
officials and tax collectors collected money for the national coffers. Money was
also collected from other administrative areas, known as Hundreds in the
south and Wapentakes in the north. The Hundreds met every four weeks in
the open air, usually at a crossroads—at a time when all roads were 'green'.

Another clue which leads back to this period came about as a result of
deforestation. During the Dark Ages, many lanes leading into woods were left
long after the wood itself had disappeared. (For further information, see the
section on hedge-dating in Chapter 4).

Place-name evidence for wooded areas can be found in the words 'leigh',
'hurst', 'bearu' and 'den'. Examples can be found in Nun's Lane in
Bedfordshire, which now forms part of the Greensand Ridge Walk and is also
a county boundary. Bruce Chatwin, author of Songlines and lifelong student of
nomads, said: "One day Aunt Ruth told me our surname had once been
'Chettewynde', which meant a winding path in Anglo-Saxon."

'Baulks', or strips of unploughed land where the oxen turned the plough,
date back to Anglo-Saxon times. Access lanes to these patterns of fields still
survive in many counties. The 'S-shaped' ploughing patterns of the Anglo-
Saxons produced a particular form of field, and lanes can still be found as
access to these.

Some lanes will date back to early Christian pilgrim routes, such as sections
of The Pilgrim's Way in Kent or The Saint's Way in Cornwall. Tracing lanes
around an existing or ruined monastery is an obvious place to start when searching for Anglo-Saxon green lanes. There may be records of what were known as
'cartullary routes', which were postal services between two religious sites.

When travelling, the presence of water along the way would have literally
been a blessing, as many wayside wells and fountains were dedicated to religious saints and martyrs. Eight percent of the riverside crossings mentioned
in the Domesday Book later became place names; the Anglo-Saxon word *brycg*

(bridge) can also refer to a causeway. River and stream crossings are mentioned 666 times in Anglo-Saxon charters.

One commodity of particular importance to the stock-owning Saxons was salt: the terms *sealpath*, *sealstræt* and *sealtrod* (saltway) occur 18 times in Anglo-Saxon charters.

It is perhaps a mistake to think that a narrow path is ancient, as by the 1500s Acts were passed to ensure that roads were wide enough for two waggons to pass, for two oxherds to make their goads touch across them, and for 16 armed knights to ride side by side along them.

Some lanes called *port stræt*, which lead to local markets, were founded in Roman times and continued to thrive into the Anglo-Saxon period.

Although predominantly peace-loving, the Anglo-Saxons were carrying on the practice of 'containing' the Celts, first begun by the Romans.

Offa's Dyke was constructed in the eighth century by the Saxon King Offa to protect his people from the Welsh, and to confirm the boundary of his Mercian Kingdom. The original dyke was supposed to be 20 feet high with a ditch 10 feet wide. Over time, sections of this 167-mile fortification have become green lanes.

Many woods (and some wood pastures) dating from the thirteenth century were fixed and protected by great earthworks: evidence of this can be found in the massive coppice-stools and ancient pollards which form part of some boundary hedges. Many 'holloways' date from this period; they once were part of routes to religious sites, markets or Manorial Courts.

The Manorial Courts which came into existence at the end of this period were responsible for the regulation of internal field boundaries, the precise amounts of grazing and the rights of gathering furze and bracken on the 'common waste' (scrub land). They also looked after trackways and streams. The creation of the

A Path Under Threat

The word 'herepath', used in Saxon times, referred to 'the broad army path' trod by warriors. In 1998 one of these paths fell under threat.

In December 1990 Thames Water had revealed plans to establish the site of a giant reservoir between the towns of Abingdon and Wantage. Running almost diagonally across the centre of it is one of Britain's most ancient but least known trackways, the old Wantage to Abingdon Bridleway, a right of way. The extinguishing of such trackways is of course regrettable but, as in the quarry case in Somerset (see page 62), inevitable when the supply of such essential requirements as food, water and shelter are concerned. However, just as in the Somerset case, maybe a consideration should have been made of the possibility of denying Londoners their extra 150,000 million litres of water (two months supply), by challenging them on whether or not they were doing their bit. Could a reduction in water use have prevented the destruction of this ancient lane?

new churches and parishes, which were a feature of the late Saxon and early Norman period, reinforced the emphasis on central settlements.

So the basic shape of our villages, and their geographical distribution, was in place by 1300. You will find a list of all the English villages which existed in *Nomina Villarum* 1316 and in the Lay Subsidy Rolls of 1334.

Another land form division recorded in the North is that of the Wapentake (from the Scandinavian word *vapnatak*), when armed warriors at a meeting would clash their swords together in agreement (a bit like the meeting of palms in brotherhood). Other divisions are Hundreds, Wards, Lathes, Rapes and Leets. Sometimes you will find green lanes leading to the meeting places associated with these divisions.

THE MEDIÆVAL AND ELIZABETHAN PERIODS

The network of roads in mediæval England was very much created by the emerging pattern of markets and fairs, to which an increasingly mobile local population demanded access. It is a good idea to get the overall picture of mediæval markets and towns by looking at Beresford and Joseph's *Mediæval England*, an aerial survey made in 1979. The site of a fair just outside a town and the roads leading to it may be traceable through green lanes.

In appearance, mediæval lanes can often be more sunken than those which date back to earlier times. Not only may they have been used on a daily basis for travel between one settlement and another, but they could have had greater use on market days.

This whole topic of mediæval fairs, including the products sold there, those who supplied them, those who attended, those who entertained there and those who regulated there, may help you trace the history of the green lane. But more than that, it will give you a feel for what was actually going on there at the time. With this economic explosion came the need for the King and his tax collectors to travel around the country on a regular basis: royal itineraries provide clues to these once important routes.

During this period, where parishes were very large it was often necessary to carry a corpse along a lychway to reach the parish church (e.g. the Lychways on Dartmoor, leading to Widecombe and Lydford).

Records of Bishop's Visitations, available in most local Records Offices, will list the settlements as well as towns and religious sites that the Bishop visited. Many powerful and rich people had chantry chapels set up in their own homes, which would have been worth a visit by the Bishop. You can build up a map of these over a present day system of lanes, and this will date any green lane still existing today.

Pilgrims lanes were deepened during this period. Those with religious monuments on the way are easily detected, such as the cross on the Mediæval Way from Leek to Macclesfield.

The various Tudor Poor Law Acts from 1601 onwards gave the responsibility for the maintenance of the roads to the poor who lived within an ancient

> ### Evidence from a Manorial Court Roll
>
> Stokenham Manor Court 25th September 1600
> Margery Putt, widow, is given until 25th March, under penalty of 5 shillings, to repair the hedge between the common road leading to her West Down and the land of Richard Shaghe.
>
> Stokenham Manor Court 10th April 1601.
> Margery Putt, widow, has repaired her hedge between the road at West Downe and the land of Richard Shaghe.

ecclesiastical parish, thus making it a civil duty (see extract in Records of Highway Maintenance in Appendix IV).

The mediæval period also saw the beginnings of 'Perambulations', set up to delineate the boundaries of forests and thus protect them from deforestation. The term for this (which you may come across in documents) is Assart Lands; the dykes and hedges, some of which still flank green lanes today, resulted from this.

An example of the implementation of Edward I's Trench Act (see Appendix IV) is to be found in an ancient woodland in the parish of Long Melford in Suffolk: Lineage Wood, about 90 acres in all, which dates back to 1386. A track running from east to west, with a wood bank on the north side, marks the edge of the original wood. There is also a length of holloway at TL88654821.

Bridges which are approached by long stretches of zigzag road indicate a route built to prevent groups of packhorses and carts stampeding out of control down the gradient towards the bridge. Those bridges which appear on green lanes and have ecclesiastically pointed arches belong to the mediæval period. Records dating from this period sometimes contain reports of ambushes and attacks which occurred at these vulnerable travel points.

As we are now entering the age of map-making, where fords, stepping stones and other crossing places feature, from this time onwards we can date the green lanes leading to them with some accuracy.

The mediæval system of strip farming gave three forms of access, all of which can still be identified today in the form of green lanes. They may lead into or be adjacent to (a) unfenced trackways, (b) Assart Lands, or (c) unenclosed waste or moorland in the north of England, and heathlands in the south.

Then there are the lanes which appear to lead nowhere, ending in the middle of a field: these were the roads which led to mediæval villages that had been deserted because of the Black Death (1348), or when families were evicted to make way for the grazing of sheep for wool during this period.

Packhorse lanes, with ledges to facilitate the passing of the loads going to and from market, may date from this period.

Although we often associate stone quarrying with the expansion in house building after the agricultural revolution, mediæval times also saw a lot of

> ### Investigating an Old Lane
>
> The main lane from Dunstable to Totternhoe is clearly very old. Eileen Roberts, writing about the stone mines at Totternhoe, says that a broad thoroughfare, Wheelbarrow Way, led from Rats Holes Pit, between Quarry Pits and Quarry Flat, across Hunger Hill. . . . Its great breadth, from 1 to 3 chains, (1 chain = 66 ft), indicates the scale of the quarrying output at its apogee . . . . Wheelbarrow Way proceeded eastwards merging with Drovers Way. . . . She also notes the large number of carts required for transporting the stone.—*Mediæval Archaeology*, Vol XVIII.

building in progress, with the founding of regional fairs and markets bringing greater prosperity to town and country.

Handwriting

When working in local or national archives, you will come across documents which are difficult to decipher because of the handwriting. Many extra-mural departments of universities run excellent courses to help out with these problems, and I have included some books on the subject in the Bibliography. The following is a summary of the different styles you may come across as you work your way through the ages of your lane.

The script known as Caroline Miniscule is found in manuscripts from the 8th to the 12th century, and appears in the Charter, Court and Book forms of handwriting. Private charters before the last decade of the 13th century are rarely dated, so recognition of this hand is a dating device in itself. The alphabet lists (see page 45) should prove helpful.

Another document which you will find useful in your searches will be the 'Feet of Fines', a record of exchanges of land which dates back to the twelfth century. The term 'feet' is used because the bottom of the document was detached as a receipt for those involved in the transaction. They can contain topographical details, which might include ancient roads. Finally, there is the physical evidence of a lane having been used by a cart or waggon: the standard distance between the axles is 4 feet 8 inches. This measurement was later adopted by the railways to define the standard ~~broad~~ gauge width of track.

DROVERS' ROADS AND PACKHORSE TRAILS

How to identify green lanes which were once drovers' ways

This checklist will help in identifying such lanes on the ground, but further research will need to be undertaken to be sure that they were once used by drovers. As always, the exact dating is difficult, but the most important period for droving was 1750–1850.

Appearance

1. Width: this can be from 20–40 yards (18–36 metres).
2. Stances or halts: these can occur within a lane itself or adjacent to the lane. They will be found where the lane opens out to provide a grazing area.
3. The lane will have very wide, tree-free verges, which were also used for grazing. In Yorkshire it has been calculated that there were a hundred acres of pasture available for cattle on the drovers' route from Scotch Corner to Bowes.
4. A walled or hedged cattle pound may appear within or at the end of the lane.
5. The length of a drovers' way is usually over half a mile, but smaller, earlier ways were used for cattle too.
6. The lane may well link up with a major road which leads into a town.
7. It may run parallel to an old turnpike route, enclosure road or another major route (although sometimes it may be well hidden).
8. It will lead in the direction of a market town or former fair, an ecclesiastical institution or a port.
9. There will be some form of water supply adjacent to or within the lane: a natural pond, dewpond, well, spring, or more unusually a trough and a pump.
10. The lane may cross a natural ford at a wide point in a river.
11. If there are Scots Pines along the way, this indicates that the landowners were well disposed to offer hospitality to Scottish drovers.
12. At minor rivers, there will be smallish, early bridges, known as packhorse bridges ('hebbles' in Derbyshire).

Place-name evidence

1. The use of drove, drift, oxway, the rothern, lode, neat, droveden, the holloway or the shieling for the lane or roads nearby.
2. Farmsteads along the way may bear such obvious names as The Halt or Drovers' Rest. If so, the fields within these farms may then be investigated. The following will give evidence of the fees charged by the farmer for grazing

Historical Use of Green Lanes

Michael Bayley, a chartered architect from Maidenhead, writes:

"I come from yeoman farming stock in the South Berks and East Berks part of the Thames valley, and am just old enough to have known the last people to use the local green lanes for their original use, of droving livestock in the 1920s and 30s. Up until the outbreak of the 39-45 war transhumance was still practised by the villagers in Burnham, Uppenham, Eton Wick, Cholney Dovney and Boveney, who sent their cattle and goats as they had always done up our green lanes, called Oldways Lane, Hogfair, Cow Piece Lane, Deep Lane and Green Lane. They sent them to Farnham Common and Burnham Beeches in the Summer to graze and browse the woodlands while the village commons and greens grew hay for winter feed."

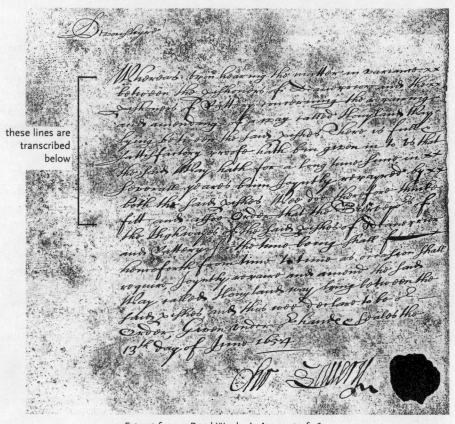

these lines are
transcribed
below

Extract from a Road Warden's Account of 1654

Dear Parishioners,
1. whosoever upon hearing this matter in warrant
2. between the parishes of Dean Prior and the
3. parishes of Rattery concerning the repairing
4. and mending of a way called Honeylands Way
5. lying between the said parish there is fully
6. satisfactory proof hath been given unto us that
7. the said Way hath for a long time since in
8. several places been jointly repaired by
9. both the said parishes who do therefore think
10. fit and agree orders that the repairs of

The text goes on in similar vein, the two parishes in agreement all the way through. The 'xxx' at the end of lines 1-4 and 7-8 have no romantic significance; they are to prevent any later additions, similar to writing 'only' on a cheque after the amount. When translating a document, it is easier to decipher line by numbered line, leaving gaps for undecipherable words within a line, to which you can return later.

(8) *Engrossing Secretary Hand:* 1658

A a bcd dee e ff g hikl ll m   no p q r ſs ſt v u w x y z et

(9) *Sloped Secretary Hand:* 1663 *(but written much earlier)*

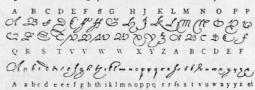

A a bcd e ee f g h th i k l m n o p p q   rr ſs s t v u w x y y z et

(10) and (11) *Mixed Hands (Round-hand): c.* 1670

A   a bc c d de e ff g h h h i ij k k l all   m n

N n op   p q q r r s ſs st v   u w w x y y z z ꝣ

A a bc c d de f g gh i k l m n o p q rst v u w x   z

(18) *Small Legal:* 1663 *(but written much earlier)*

A A a a a B Bbbb C C Cccc D D dd ꝺ E eꝺꝼ ꝼ

ff ff f f f Gg gꝼg hhh J ii jj k k ꝃ k l l ll M M nuñ

miñ N inn inñ N O ooo P P p p p p Q Qq q q̃ꝺ q R Rr r

S Sss ſſ ſt Tt tꝺ Vu v W W W x x x y y z z ꝣ

ALPHABET OF DIFFERENT SCRIPTS

If you familiarize yourself with the appearance of the words which refer to high-ways and roads in general this will help in your scan reading of a document. For example, during the Saxon period the thorn was used on a regular basis and appears in Charters in words such as cyric-paꝥ (church path: thorn = ꝥ). In subsequent documents the word 'way' is often used in connection with roads. As you will see from the charts, the letter 'w' has had a flamboyant history.

> ### Definitions from John Richardson's Encyclopædia
>
> *Green Lane;* Sometimes synonymous with a Driftway. As its name implies it is a grassed road, probably leading to market. A right of way.
> *Drift/Drove Roads;* Ancient roads which were not subject to toll, and used mainly for long distance herding of cattle.
>
> (With thanks to David Inglesant of Puttenham, Guildford)

(but they may also refer to the size and value of the field): Half Penny, Farthing, Penfold, Pinfold, and Booths in the Vale of Edale, Derbyshire.

3. Public houses and inns also reveal the presence of drovers, such as The Shepherd and Dog, The Drovers' Arms, The Black Bull and The Fiddlers—a popular way for Scottish drovers to pass the time. Place name evidence may also appear incorporating geese or hogs, e.g. The Boar's Head.

4. Names such as The Blacksmith's Arms and The Farrier also show their presence; and look out for The Old Smithy as a private house name. The same applies for the evidence of tanneries (e.g. Tanpits Lane). As in 3 above, it is the position of these pubs which will reveal their use to drovers: for example The Travellers Rest at Epping Green is situated strategically outside the London markets and within early morning striking distance of Epping itself.

5. One of the longest shots to provide evidence of drovers is to be found in the hair which was used to bind lath and plaster together in old barns by the wayside. Is it the hair of a Highland, Welsh or Yorkshire breed?

Written evidence

The routes taken by licensed Corn and Dairy Merchants or itinerant merchants (known as badgers), can often be found in Records Offices under Quarter Sessions. There are also Trade Directories (available in most large local libraries and published yearly); newspaper advertisements; archive photographs; Tithe Maps (useful for giving individual field names—many Women's Institutes took part in field-naming studies in the 1970s).

Another useful source outlining ways and highways is 'The Glebe Terriers', traceable from 1697. The terriers referred to here are not the ones kept for hunting, but the territorial rights of the parish, which may include tracks and rights of way.

If it can be proved that a green lane was once a Drovers' Way, can this be beneficial in preserving its status? The right to drive animals over land was always part of highway law until 1981. If only this right existed in regard to a particular lane (as opposed to rights being given to carriages and wheeled vehicles), then it can be argued that it is not appropriate to reclassify an old Drovers' Way as a Byway Open to All Traffic (BOAT), as it was not so in the past. This argument does not always hold up, as new laws can sometimes affect the implementation of old ones. (For further discussion on this, see the section entitled 'Nothing to Crow About' in Chapter 5.)

GREEN LANES IN THE INDUSTRIAL AGE

The Enclosure Acts of the eighteenth century were brought in to increase agricultural production, in order to provide food for those involved in industrial production. They were designed to enlarge fields, just as intensive farming practices today have done. In the process, the lanes which led to the smaller fields often disappeared; only a few survive as green lanes.

During this period, one-fifth of the English countryside changed its appearance, with the majority of the Acts taking place in the Midlands. The Acts gave strict instructions concerning how this new landscape was to be created:

Public Carriage roads to be fenced on both Sides, and no Gates to be erected thereon or Trees planted within 50 yards of each other on either sides thereof.

From this it is plain to see that Enclosure was accompanied by a good deal of deforestation (just as with field expansion schemes from the 1940s onward).

When tracing Enclosure Act green lanes on the ground, their surface may well be a very stony one, as described below:

The roads are to be covered with stone 12' wide, being 17" thick in the middle and 5" thick at the outside.

Although trees were grubbed out and the fencing of the wide lanes was easily done by a wealthy landowner, the more slow-growing and more stock-proof planting of a monoculture 'quickset' (hawthorn) hedge can also be an indicator that the lane dates back to this period. You will find Enclosure Acts in the Ecclesiastical Records section of the Records Office and in the individual Parish lists files, but there is probably a central list within the Records Office (so you won't have to go through every Parish file).

Occupational lanes and those used for access to mines are as varied as the minerals which were extracted during the Industrial Revolution. Here is a list of industrial activities which may well have green lanes still leading to their ruins today (based on the English Heritage listing):

• Lead, coal, slate, alum, stone lime, gunpowder, tin, clay, arsenic and barytes, and for the processes leading to the production of glass, iron, steel, brass and cement.
• Lanes which lead to lime kilns often remain green today, and are a remnant of agricultural practices associated periods prior to the agricultural revolution.
• Those leading to sites for the production of electric power, ice (houses), water, sewage treatment, salt, oil, gas and metal workings.
• Those leading to old engineering sites, hydraulic rams, disused bridges and early construction sites.
• Those which are approach roads to activities in the countryside, such as the extraction of inorganic chemicals and organic chemicals, timber, peat production (turbury) paths, rural kilns and those associated with gamekeeping or hunting.

• Those associated with food production: corn milling and drying, brewing and distilling, other organic agricultural products and the textile industry.
• Those leading to sites of human, animal, water and wind power, combustion engines, roadways, railways, inland waterways, sea, coast and air transport communications.

The Industrial Revolution brought with it a revolution in the mobility of the population: when huge population shifts occurred, old lanes saw more human traffic along them.

The first Turnpike Act was passed in 1663; by 1821, over 18,000 miles (29,000 kilometres) of English roads had been turnpiked, i.e. become toll-paying. The word derives from 'turn-spike', which was a pole set up in the road to prevent travellers from passing.

Turnpike Acts at the local level are available for inspection in the House of Commons Library. Although the preamble and form are set, you can often find references to lanes in the first paragraphs of the Acts, which show you exactly where the road once ran—and maybe the green lane still shows this.

Then there are the positions of toll houses, booths and gates along a route. You may find that a green lane marks a back route to them—a way of sneaking past the keeper. Because the original papers relating to Turnpikes were sometimes deposited with solicitors, it is worth looking into the vaults of your local long-established firms to find details of the routes and maps.

In Records Offices, Turnpike Acts are listed under 'Official Records of Other Authorities'.

Quarter Sessions

A wealth of documents can be found here. The procedure is that when you enter a Records Office you first consult the files which will give you details of what is available in the vaults. You then order up your documents by entering the number of the document on a docket. You sit silently, armed with a pencil, at a large table set for you to unroll your evidence upon. Then up it comes in a cardboard vault box. It may be wrapped in pink document ribbon too—enjoy! However many documents you order up, you can be sure that just five minutes before the Records Office is due to close you will find what you've been looking for all day.

Turnpike Acts and Deposited Plans will provide the best sources for researching green lanes but remember that records contained in Quarter Session papers will vary from County to County.

Milestones

Official milestones went up along the London to Chester Road in 1744, the year of the first Parliamentary Act which authorized them on main roads. Those which followed obviously reflected Turnpike routes, and by the 1830s some 20,000 miles of roads were obliged to have stones at one mile intervals along the road. As has been explained, some of these can be found along stretches of today's green lanes which once formed part of these Turnpikes (see box on page 36).

Living memory testimonies

These are one of your greatest resources when researching lanes. Not only will locals remember having walked the lanes, but they will know why they did so, and where the lanes connected with others. They will have walked, cycled and ridden along the lanes with a purpose other than recreation.

In the colour plate section there is a picture of horizontal and wire bar fencing. This could have been put in by workers on conscript labour schemes between 1918 and 1938. The workers had a choice at the end of the day to be paid either 10s 6d (52½p), or to receive a food parcel.

Matching documentary evidence with physical evidence

It's not enough just to feel that a lane should be preserved because it is ancient, or because it seems to follow part of an old drovers' way or saltway; there must be criteria which will back up these feelings, and give weight to arguments for their preservation.

If green lanes are to be preserved because of their historical importance, then we need to know how this importance is recognized by an official body such as English Heritage. In 1990, EH published a Monuments Protection Programme, by which 'Single Monuments' such as roads might be judged.

Below are some of the criteria used in the selection of monuments of national importance. These refer to mediæval roads, many of which are green lanes.

- *Survival*
- *Group value*—associated with various monuments such as brickworks, bridges, castles, chapels, churches, deserted villages, field systems, frontier works, glassworks, inhabited villages, ironworks, lime kilns, manors, markets, moats, monasteries, peletowers, potteries, palaces, quarries, salt-works, shrunken villages, tile kilns, tower houses, towns, trackways, watermills and windmills. English Heritage rates lanes with six of these monuments as having a high value; those with five or four, medium value; and those with three or below, low value.
- *Documentation—archæological*. Alignment/Excavation.
- *Documentation—historical*. Road-names, the Parish Map, the Gough Map, various itineraries, Court Rolls, trade accounts, Close Rolls, Patent Rolls, toll schedules, building accounts, the Hundred Rolls, ministers' accounts, and in contemporary literature. The score here is two or more good, one medium and none poor.
- *Potential*. The main contexts for the preservation of artefactual, ecofactual and environmental evidence are the matrix of the road, the road surface, the fills of the drains, the fills of ditches, the buried land surface, the riverine deposits at fords.
- *Diversity*. The main components of roads are, the road surface, kerbs, drains, ditches, central gullies, zigzags, causeways, fords and junctions.

Sites which have evidence of three or more components may be scored
high; with two only, medium; and one or none, low.

• *Amenity value*. Many mediæval roads are still in use today as footpaths,
bridal paths or farm tracks, roads which are still a public right of way which
are of educational or recreational use and where the alignment is visible, in
some form, across the landscape may be scored high. Sites with limited
access but where the alignment of the road is visible from ground level may
be scored 'medium'. Sites with no public access and/or which leave no
visible traces at ground level may be scored low.

Although this document is useful in identifying what English Heritage calls a
'mediæval road', it goes on to state that there seems to be little hope for their
conservation. In some cases it suggests that a buffer zone should be left alongside stretches of roads which include holloways and their adjacent drainage features and boundary ditches. Whether this would become part of a greenfield or
a brownfield site is a matter for debate, as indeed are all the English Heritage
criteria, but they may prove useful in your discussions with local authorities
about a particular green lane which you wish to preserve or excavate.

It is virtually impossible to list all the sources available for researching lane
history, but with the help of your local Records Office, the relevant Ist Series
1:250,000 OS map and some of the books listed in the bibliography, you should
be well on the way to discovering more about your lane's use through the ages.

Aerial photographs are another useful source for lane dating. Also, refer to
the methodology for research based on studies made in East Sussex (see
Appendix IV).

This one leads down to the water's edge
to the stream, the river, the tide.
This one smells of seaweed
and the salt tears of the widowed bride.

As long as the length of the Green Lane
is the story it will confide.

This one crosses the Roman bridge
where the causeway is now buried deep.
this one has no zigzags
which the Romans considered a cheat!

As long as the length of the Green Lane
is the story it will repeat.

This one curves round fields
of barley, fat hen and rye.
This one passes the headland
where Saxon oxen bones lie.

As long as the length of the Green Lane
is the story it will cry.

This one leads to the silent field
where the mediæval fair once pitched.
this one is protected
by its robber-proof stinking ditch.

As long as the length of the Green Lane
is the story it will reach.

This one is wide and bullock proof
with wider still pine-ringed glades.
This one is where the drovers
walked away their working days.

As long as the length of the Green Lane
is the story it will say.

This one is short and blackish
and leads to the fenced pit head.
This one is in memory
of industries long since dead.

As long as the length of the Green Lane
is the story it will thread.

This one is starved amidst plenty
where cars, lorries, buses all go.
this one is a dog-walker's bike-ride
where children play safely in snow.

As long as the length of the Green Lane
is the story which to you it can show.

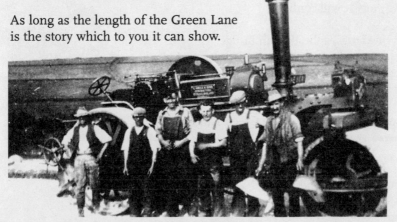

A 1920s tarmacking gang—about to change the appearance of green lanes for ever.

COMMON TREES TO BE FOUND IN GREEN LANES

A cross-section of a typical sunken green lane, showing some of the trees found. For flora to be found in a green lane, see Appendix III.

Ash	Hawthorn
Beech	Hazel
Blackthorn	Holly
Briar	Honeysuckle
Common Dog Rose	Oak
Dogwood	Sycamore
Elm	Sweet Chestnut
Elder	Wych Elm

Chapter Four

THE ECOLOGY
OF GREEN LANES

"Come with me this last April the old lane may know. These wildings know nothing of their doom: now is their hour of sunshine. The flowers of the black-thorn are already tinged with brown, the petals are falling; the leaves breaking green from their last buds. That long grey-green, slow-worm-like cable rising from the hedge, and fallen, coiled with its own weight, is the head of the wood-bine, which will be an inch longer on our return this afternoon. . . . A little bit of bread and no chee-ee-se—there sits the yellowhammer, uttering its weak little song, its rillet of wild music, which the hungry ploughboys of long ago used for their own complaint. Thyme grows at the edge of the rock, with the rest-harrow, whose small flowers, like pink sweet-peas, will come in June, with the blossoms of the lovely scented ploughman's spikenard. Lovely wildflower names, so proper in the old lane."—Henry Williamson, *The Lone Swallows* (1930), describing Vention Lane at Putsborough Sands in north Devon.

There is something positively tropical about this description of the wildlife in a sunken Devonshire lane. Could it be true that woodbine tendrils grow at the rate of an inch a day, or was that just back in 1930? Whether true or not it doesn't really matter, because what is being described is the untamed nature of a wildlife corridor which survives untouched by the casual intrusions of man. It is these casual intrusions, the ones not motivated by commerce or social obligation, which have always been such a threat to green lanes.

I once led a group of walkers on a 'wild food foray'. In order to reach the site where the collecting and cooking would take place, a green lane had to be traversed. Unfortunately, people could not desist from collecting edible plants and asking questions along the length of the lane, so that by the time the site was reached a large part of what we had planned to do there had to be abandoned. The walkers had become engrossed by the complexity and biodiversity of the green lane. These wildlife corridors have so much to give; they are convenient corridors to step into at any

Restharrow

Ploughman's
Spikenard

time of the year and observe in great detail. Whether they be deep in the countryside or adjacent to towns, we cannot afford to lose them.

When surveying green lanes, many councils and interest groups include information on the adjacent use of land; for although there is wildlife living within and along the lane, there are other creatures which come in on an occasional, daily, nocturnal, even seasonal basis. The occupants are forever changing.

WILDLIFE AND THE LANE

Seat yourself at the centre of this cross-habitat corridor, and wait for the sun to come up. On the ground it will be damp and cold, and the slugs and snails are ready to retreat to the verges and ditches of the lane. Moths will already have folded their wings and hidden in the foliage. The lane faces east–west, and the sun will first filter through the densely leaved foliage above, and begin to warm the breasts of the small birds who have been roosting at mid-hedge level all night. Wrens rustle along their linear caves. If it is autumn, cobwebs glint and reveal the spider at the centre for finches, tits, and buntings to pick off. In the warming air some midges emerge, and on the top branches thrushes and blackbirds begin to sing, keeping their eyes on the midgey haze and watching for the first butterflies to flit along the lane. Down below in the banks, voles become busy searching for insects to feed upon. As the sun's rays creep up the side of the tunnel, fern fronds straighten; herb robert flowers, always in bloom, begin to open up. At the base of the hedge, scarlet pimpernels open, but only until mid-day. Now come the bigger birds—great tits, swallows and pigeons—streaking down the centre; a badger finally retreats into his sett at the top of the bank, a flurry of dirty bedding pushed down in front of him. Squirrels liven up the proceedings by leaping from the now fully sunned branches at one side of the lane to the other side—like rainforest monkeys.

Rabbits bask in a patch of sunlight which falls through a gap in the hedge; a fieldmouse scuttles from the cold side to the warm and out into the field beyond. When the sun is overhead, the lane hums with insect life and birds whizz along the centre—swifts cut through the air. Bullfinches, song thrushes, yellowhammers, green finches and long-tailed tits, swooping in from over the fields, all fill the lane with activity.

Buzzards alternate from glowering high up on a standard oak in the hedge to soaring and circling over the tunnel to get a better view of the pantry spread out below.

A bloody-nosed beetle comes into your vision; he has started his slow crossing of the lane's surface, hoping that he will not need to put on his great display of being wounded, should any predators cross him.

In the verges, uncomfortable from the heat, frogs jump further into the damp at the sunless bottom of ditches. A pheasant may misjudge its flight and land noisily in the centre; panicked, it

Bluebell

will strut and search for escape before wheeling like an overweight jumbo jet, up and out of the tunnel again.

After noon, as the sun descends, the life on the west side increases, but is gradually eclipsed by the fading light as moths take to the wing again. Knowing of their runs, bats emerge, and once more the silence of the lane allows you to listen to their clattering wings cutting past your ears. Owls begin to call from lane to copse and, according to season, the barking of a fox may echo down from the hillside. Glow-worms glint in the hedge, and in the muddy wheel-tracks of the lane.

All this time, at the centre of the green lane tunnel, life revolves around you. As you rise to leave, treading over leaf litter teaming with life invisible to us, the night shift begins. A green lane never sleeps.

Within their microclimate, green lanes—as man-made corridors between equally man-made habitats—produce and protect their own biodiversity.

Although they clearly vary from district to district, it is safe to say that most hedgerows are habitats for half of our twenty British mammals. Plant varieties number as many as 600; and over 65 bird species have been recorded both nesting and hunting. They need insects to feed upon: over 1,500 varieties are available. One standing oak tree alone contains over 280 species of insect.

But the larder is continually being replenished as well as emptied. The corridors act as transportation routes for the dispersal of seeds, fruits and berries, coming and going just as human freight does. Shrubs and trees thrive in the habitat of green lanes. Caterpillars feed on the grasses and plants at the base of the lane, and lizards, slow worms, frogs and toads live in the ditches. If a lane has stone walls, then a whole new range of species of plant, insect, mammal and bird life will move in.

* * * * *

It's easy to get caught up in working out legal definitions for lanes, and finding out what they were used for and by whom—but to each of us our idea of a green lane is determined by where we live, where we first stumbled into one. They are all about discovery, about getting lost in a familiar landscape. The various types of landscape in the United Kingdom create different habitats and therefore are used by different species.

The Hedgerow Survey Form, which you will find on page 96, provides a good base from which to start. It lists common species, to which you can add your own regional varieties. For example, should you be lucky enough to spot a rare brown hairstreak butterfly in your lane, its presence could be due to blackthorn, as this butterfly lays its eggs on last year's blackthorn shoots. Because a green lane is so self-contained, it is possible to make such detailed studies of the interdependency of species. We have added extra columns to the form, which should help you in your survey work.

Specialist studies

The figure of 1,500 insects was mentioned above; this will give you some idea of the detail you can go into when discovering the flora and fauna of a lane. It is obviously not the purpose of this book to list all these varieties, but as an example of just what is available and where it might lead you, we have included in Appendix III some fern listings from a specialist book on the subject. As you study green lanes, and maybe specialize in the butterflies, plants or birds therein, I hope that you will come across such treasures to help you in your research.

Mammals

Just as birds use green lanes to hunt along, colonies of bats use them for the same purpose. Because moths, butterflies and many species of fly live in hedgerows, it is obvious that this should be the case. Dusk is the time to look out for them; maybe emerging from a nearby barn or building, or from their roosts in trees and shrubs along the lane. The varieties most likely to be found in green lanes are Noctules, Barbastelles and Bechstein's. Natterer's, Pipistrelles and Daubenton's are also summer feeders in lanes. Unfortunately they are not easy to identify, but here are a few clues for some of the 12 species once batting around the UK.

Daubenton's, the water bat, prefers some standing water to hunt over, and should you get close enough, is particularly furry. The Noctule, otherwise known as the Great Bat (much loved by Gilbert White, author of *The Natural History of Selborne*), is the first out in the twilight, and feeds furiously—it can eat a fourth of its own weight in one foray, its favourite moths being the Cinnabars. It has a cricket-like voice, and flies all year round.

The Barbastelle is the slenderest of the species; Bechstein's have big ears. The Pipistrelle is also known as the common bat, and has a 8" wing span; the largest wing span, at 13", belongs to the Greater Horseshoe. The Natterer can be distinguished by its red-grey colour.

From wolves to water voles, deer to dormice, bats to badgers, there are no restrictions on animals who use green lanes: no TROs (Traffic Restriction Orders) are ever served on them.

Animal tracks

Once again, it is not the intention of this book to give a detailed study of the tracks and signs left by those who cross and traverse green lanes, but the box opposite shows the tracks of some of the most common inhabitants.

Green lanes grasses

Many species of grasses can be found at different levels of a green lane; here are some clues as to what you might find.

Meadows were traditionally cut for hay in June or July, as this gave time for early summer species such as cuckoo-flower and cowslip to set seed before the cutting. Grasses in lanes adjacent to meadows may include Yorkshire fog, timothy, meadow foxtail, cocksfoot and perennial ryegrass. Waterlogged lanes

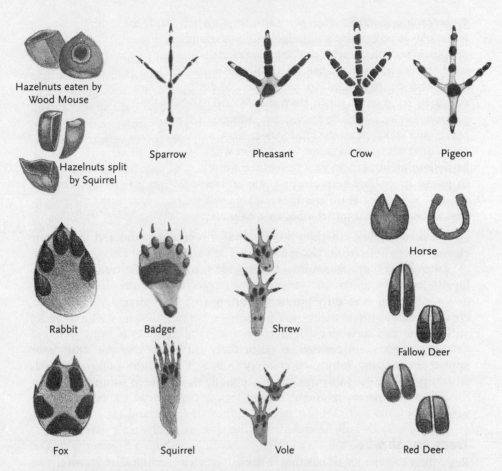

Hazelnuts eaten by Wood Mouse

Hazelnuts split by Squirrel

Sparrow

Pheasant

Crow

Pigeon

Rabbit

Badger

Shrew

Horse

Fox

Squirrel

Vole

Fallow Deer

Red Deer

may include such grasses as sweet vernal, Yorkshire fog, meadow fescue and crested dogstail, as well as rushes and sedges. Ridge and Furrow lanes, which gave access to such old open field systems, can contain meadow foxtail, meadow oat, quaking grass and timothy, and such herbs as betony and knapweed. Downland, where established on chalk, is an infertile environment; it produces perennials such as quaking grass, cocksfoot, sheep's fescue, red fescue and meadow oat.

Scrub

This is pioneer woody growth, spanning the transition period from open ground to woodland cover, and therefore likely to be found in a neglected green lane. It is made up of shrubs growing naturally on the particular soil of an area: hawthorn, hazel, elder on the heavier soils, birch and

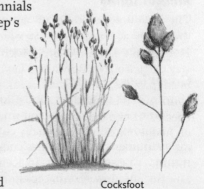

Cocksfoot

gorse on lighter soils, interspersed as time goes by with the young trees which will form an indigenous woodland, if people do not intervene. It can be found stretching back behind green lanes which border on heathland or moorland in particular, and needs to be kept in check both inside and outside the lane. Before taking any action, make sure you consult the landowners first.

Crested Dogtail

Armed with a good flower guide, you will be able to identify most varieties which grow in green lanes. But here are just one or two species to look for at different levels, some of which have come from neighbouring habitats.

• Cuckoo-flower, cowslip, yellow rattle, oxeye daisy and red and white clovers creeping in from meadows.

• Ragged robin, meadowsweet and great burnet may be found in waterlogged lanes.

• Orchids such as early purple flowering, rock rose, thyme, salad burnet, lady's bedstraw, dwarf thistle and plantains are found in lanes with a chalky subsoil and also on verges.

• Cow wheat—an interesting plant. I do not know why the word 'cow' appears in its name, but maybe it is a degeneration of wheat, as the tiny seeds which the flower produces were once sought by the poor and ground into flour.

• The climbers—old man's beard, bryony and ivy—all thrive in the hedgerows.

Trees and shrubs

Regarding the matter of naming different species, I think that knowing the names of the trees is less important than recognizing the differences between them. Besides the standard broadleaved trees, there are many guides which will identify the more unusual varieties such as dogwood, spindle, and the Wayfaring Tree.

Hedge-dating

The following method of dating a hedge (and therefore a lane) was pioneered by Dr. Max Hooper and Dr. E. Pollard. Much of the research was carried out in Devon and East Anglia, but has been proven valid for all areas of the UK. By counting the number of different hardwood species of tree on one side of a 30-metre stretch of hedgerow, it is possible to calculate in hundreds the age of the hedge. This is a rule of thumb—the calculations can be given more accuracy by following the rules set out in the *Collins Guide to Hedges* (see Bibliography).

Perennial Ryegrass

In the absence of shrubs on acid hedgebanks, bramble-dating can be used instead. In this case you count the number of different species of bramble (and there are over 300), which will give you an idea of how old the lane is.

Insect life

Of the 1,500 available, you must find your own favourites. One of mine is the Harvest Man (the commonest orb-spider, which is a spinner and called *Meta degmentata*); the other is the garden or diadem spider (*Araneus diadematus*), with a white cross on her back. Wolf spiders lurk in walls, spinning their dense, tunnel-like webs to blend in with the stones. In muddy lanes in July and August, you may be lucky enough to spot the pin-dot lights of glow-worms. Dragonflies and damsel-flies are always to be seen around puddles of standing water and ditches in green lanes; they obviously use them as flight paths to get from one water source to another.

Snail-dating

A word about snails. There are many varieties, and it is said that they will help date a lane whose surface is composed of a particular kind of stone: for example the tiles used by the Romans, or a limestone surface. When you find empty shells of one species in large quantities, it could indicate that a lane used to run that way.

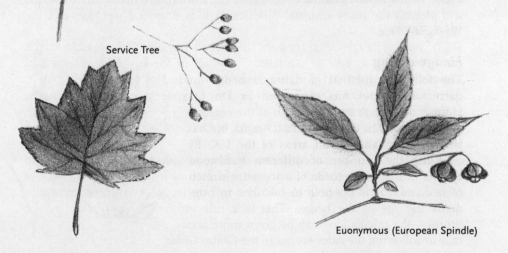

Arum Lily

Bush Vetch

Red Campion

Service Tree

Euonymous (European Spindle)

Birds

One of the most dangerous times to enter a green lane is shortly after the swifts arrive. These birds, with their sculptured, set-back wings, sweep along at such a rate, scooping up all the midges and flies in their flight path that you may well find yourself being treated in the same way.

Long-tailed tits, with their swooping movements, hunting along the outside of a lane, are easily recognizable by their whistling chatter. In autumn they make for the brown dock seeds, alder cones, sycamore and ash wings. Their swirlings have given them the appropriate collective noun of 'charm', which is applied to all finches.

Starlings can also behave in this manner when they are gathering in what is known as a 'murmuration' along the hedgerow fields by green lanes.

Lapwings, curlew and snipe use the estuary and coastal lanes during the summer breeding season. Hedgerows provide obvious nesting sites for many different birds, and they occupy 'flats' on different floors. Buzzards, kestrels and owls all use the top storey, which they are sometimes forced to share with 'buildings' of rooks and 'unkindnesses' of ravens—although it is actually the buzzards who are unkind in the spring, when they do their best to destroy the ravens' eggs. The middle levels belong to screeching jays and drumming woodpeckers, calmed and soothed by the pigeons with whom they co-exist. The lower levels of a hedgerow and the scrub are occupied by wrens (in 'herds'), tits, siskins and finches.

At any time of the year it is possible to disturb pheasants strutting in the lanes. They take to the air in ungainly flight, but their undercarriages usually clear the hedgerows. See the Red Data List for birds in Appendix III.

Practical conservation measures

In Chapter 6 ('How to Get Involved') you will find information on working in green lanes, but here are just some of the environmental considerations to bear in mind before you start.

Hedgerows

Don't work on hedgerows during the birds' breeding season, from early March until August. It is best to cut back vegetation in the lanes (i.e. plants and flowers—not shrubs and trees) twice per annum: in May or June and again in August or September. If this can only be done on an annual basis, then August is the month to choose.

The autumn is another critical period, berry crops being an invaluable food supply for birds and mammals.

Hedges should be cut every two or three years, so they do not fall into neglect. If you leave them longer, you will incur a lot more costs by way of labour and machinery (at least half as much again, according to government research).

Verges

Where a green lane opens out at a gateway or a junction with another road, a rich variety of flora and fauna can be found on the verges. To maintain the species diversity, cutting for hay is best done in early spring. Alternatively, cut from mid-June to July (the timing depending on weather conditions). Such timing of cuts allows species to flower and set seed, and causes minimal disturbance to ground nesting birds.

Remember that under Section 11 of the Countryside Act 1968, authorities should endeavour to safeguard wildlife, and also geologically and physiographically important features.

Keeping the lanes green

If you're lucky enough to live in an Area of Outstanding Natural Beauty (AONB) or close to a Site of Special Scientific Interest (SSSI), you may find that the green lanes in those areas are automatically protected as biodiverse wildlife corridors.

The new Countryside & Rights of Way Act (CROW) has made provision for footpaths and bridleways within AONBs and those which have high wildlife value to be protected by Traffic Restriction Orders (TROs).

Test Case for the Preservation of Tree Roots

The case of the green lane at Backwell Farleigh, Flax Bourton in the Wraxall area in Somerset (ST501694-ST502709), is presenting planners with some serious problems. Tarmac plc have applied to build a mile and a half long conveyor belt across Green Belt land to a disused MOD railway track, in order to ship aggregate by rail to the South East of England instead of by lorry. This of course is commendable, as it will take freight off the road. But the conveyor belt is running alongside the hedgerow of a sunken green lane which is a RUPP and a Parish Boundary.

The environmental considerations which need to be upheld here illustrate that the 1-metre cutting and 'bunding' will undercut and cover the roots and kill the hedgerow and the oak tree (see illustration). Where additional replanting is recommended, it is noted that there is not room enough for graded planting, which according to English Nature would preserve the existence and ecology of the hedgerow.

I find this case, as with so many others since records began, to rest on long-term environmental and economic considerations. I will not be thanked for saying that in the long term the environment as a whole might benefit by letting this development go ahead. A lot of long-term projections need to be made in this case, taking into account the following considerations:

1) The amount of CO_2 involved in transporting the stone by road.
2) The amount of CO_2 involved in transporting the stone by rail.
3) The cost of re-routing the passage of the stone across the fields to the railway so as not to disturb the lane.
4) The amount of short term environmental damage involved in damaging the hedgerow and the tree.
5) Whether the damage is irreversible.
6) Whether an arrangement can be reached between the contractor and the planners to ensure that the former will make good the damage caused.

These seem harsh, but we are talking about a citizen's right to shelter, and to roam in the countryside. Which is more pressing? In this case, could there even be some kind of pledge made by the citizens who will occupy the homes made from this stone to make good the damage—a payback scheme perhaps? As tracks, lanes, roads, motorways have all brought us closer together, surely we can also take more responsibility for the damage to the environment which cases such as this cause?

The above is an example of environment versus economics, and is just one of many raging about green lanes throughout the country.

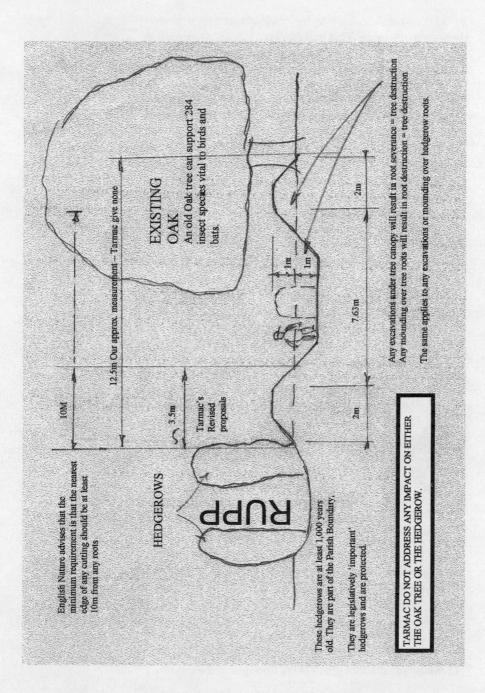

English Nature advises that the minimum requirement is that the nearest edge of any cutting should be at least 10m from any roots

10M

12.5m Our approx. measurement – Tarmac give none

EXISTING OAK

An old Oak tree can support 284 insect species vital to birds and bats.

3.5m

Tarmac's Revised proposals

HEDGEROWS

RUPP

1m

1m

7.63m

2m

2m

These hedgerows are at least 1,000 years old. They are part of the Parish Boundary.

They are legislatively 'important' hedgerows and are protected.

Any excavations under tree canopy will result in root severance = tree destruction

Any mounding over tree roots will result in root destruction = tree destruction

The same applies to any excavations or mounding over hedgerow roots.

TARMAC DO NOT ADDRESS ANY IMPACT ON EITHER THE OAK TREE OR THE HEDGEROW.

THE GREEN LANES GOURMET

Another great discovery to be made about green lanes is their culinary value. This wouldn't have been a surprise to our ancestors, who would tend special hedges for their herbal value, or for their autumn fruit-bearing varieties.

Who hasn't been blackberrying in a green lane, and been thankful for its traffic-free existence—and grateful for being able to fall back into the opposite hedgerow, as you stretch your arms and sticks up to greedily pot the plumpest without losing your balance? Our ancestors used green lanes as food stores, and so can you. At various times of year you can always find ingredients in green lanes to add to the three basic recipes below: Stir-Fries, Yoghurt Dips and Green Lanes Salads.

Pignut

Stir-fries

Use sliced quantities of the following, frying in a shallow quantity of oil. There is obviously more to fry in the autumn.

Sweet chestnuts, hazel nuts and *walnuts* are easy enough to find. The roots of the giant leaved *burdock*, sliced like water chestnuts, are very tasty; search for their feathery foliage in shady areas. *Pignut corms* taste very similar to hazel nuts, and are so small that you will be better off cooking them whole. Be careful to dig well below the leaf level before levering them up; they are well buried, and are the English answer to truffles! I am not qualified to give safe advice on the use of wild fungi, but know that *bracket fungus* and *wild field mushrooms* are perfectly suited to a stir-fry.

Dips

The following fruits can be added to *yoghurt, cream* or *fromage frais* (none of which will be found in green lanes, although maybe the ancestor of the cow from whom the dairy product is taken did once pass that way). It is said that if you find a quantity of *nettles* growing in a lane you are sure to find bones, and these may well be bones of diseased cattle slaughtered before they got to market along the drover's route. But just enjoy what is available to put in the dips in summer and autumn. There are *wild raspberries* and *strawberries, bulaces* (wild plums), *cherries, crab apples, medlars, black-berries, rowan berries* and *elderberries.*

Bullace

Wild Strawberry

Highbury Fields, Redbrook, Monmouthshire. This is a sunken
way (Cocksbury Lane) which runs through the wood.

Langber Lane Plantation, Long Preston, Settle (see page 18)

A green lane leading to a deserted ruin (left), which has since been made habitable (right)

Patterson's map is an example of an 18th century map, when all roads and lanes were green. By process of elimination and reference to more detailed and local maps, you can find out which lanes have survived into the 21st century.

Interesting discoveries to be be made in green lanes *Clockwise from top left:* Horizontal wire & bar fencing, often found at entrances to green lanes (see page 49); Old windmill at top of green lane; an example of access problems; a 'C' stone, which indicates distance from a bridge (see page 111); dry bridge—the lane is on top of the bridge, and gives access to both fields; an historic highway monument at the end of a lane.

Top: Repairing a dry stone wall near Widecombe-in-the-Moor, Dartmoor, Devon, September 2000. Photo: © Apex Photography.
Bottom: Clearing a bridleway from encroaching pines. Little Wittenham Nature Reserve, South Oxfordshire, July 1990.
Photo: Rob Bowker/BTCV.

Top left: Drainage is always a problem in green lanes. These volunteers enjoyed digging the deepest ditch possible.
Top right: Conservation volunteers staking a large pleacher in a previously neglected hedge in Stantondale, North Yorkshire, Christmas 1994. Photo: Alan Atkinson/BTCV *Bottom:* Stile repairs on a BTCV Conservation Holiday in the Forest of Bowland AONB, Lancashire, 1995. Photo: Robert Edmondson/BTCV

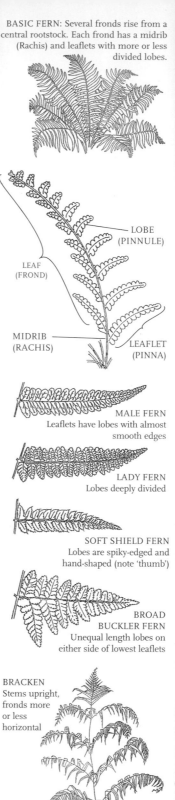

BASIC FERN: Several fronds rise from a central rootstock. Each frond has a midrib (Rachis) and leaflets with more or less divided lobes.

LOBE
(PINNULE)

LEAF
(FROND)

MIDRIB
(RACHIS)

LEAFLET
(PINNA)

MALE FERN
Leaflets have lobes with almost smooth edges

LADY FERN
Lobes deeply divided

SOFT SHIELD FERN
Lobes are spiky-edged and hand-shaped (note 'thumb')

BROAD BUCKLER FERN
Unequal length lobes on either side of lowest leaflets

BRACKEN
Stems upright, fronds more or less horizontal

Top: Lady Fern
Bottom: Hart's Tongue Fern.

Top: Soft Shield Fern
Bottom: Black Spleenwort

Salads

It is possible to make up a salad at any time of the year from the verges, hedge-banks and walls of green lanes. There are *dandelion leaves, sorrel's tender kidney shaped leaves* with their savoury taste of salt and vinegar, *young hawthorn shoots* in spring (known as bread and cheese). *Ivy-leaved toad flax*, gripping on to walls, tastes peppery, and the superb *pennywort leaves*, which can be any size from medallions to cents, go well in a cheese sandwich as a substitute for cucumber.

Other easily obtained ingredients for wild food recipes

There are *nettles* from which soup can be made; *fat hen*, a prolific and delicious early spring green; *wild hops* to flavour other herbal teas with; herbal remedies available from the aspirin content of *willow bark*; *wild marjoram, mints, rosemary* and *feverfew*, all available in green lanes hedgerows.

Fat Hen

In past times (and certainly in keeping with the practice of using a hedgerow as a larder), in a clay-soil district, people would trap and bake a hedgehog in clay.

Remember that the recipes given above are more in the nature of pruning than stripping bare, which would only lead to the demise of the lane—and prosecution for you.

Chapter Five

USE THEM OR LOSE THEM

TRYST

When drops on buds are tinkers' glasses
And sturdy boughs a nuptial arch might make,
When the ground is as true as shortbread and
The broken-belted humble bee rides by,
Cows all laden can make you late for love
Beneath the beech where the green lanes meet,
By the ford's bend where Wendy Greenway waits.
—Nick Shirley (former Green Lanes Project worker)

Waywardens first kept records relating to roads in mediæval times (and haywards looked after hedges). Some examples of the duties they performed—and the problems they had to cope with on low or non-existent budgets—are included in Chapter 3, which covers the historical development of the lanes.

Apart from the matter of remuneration, there are similarities between their responsibilities and those of today's lengthmen. This office was once common in every parish, but only a few counties can afford to employ them today. This is a great loss, for they had detailed local knowledge of the wildlife of a lane, and of how to keep the surface as clear of water as possible so all might pass through. They would have known who used a lane, for how long it had been used, and why.

Their job was a little like painting the Forth Bridge; no sooner did they have one group of Rights of Way under control, than problems would occur again at the beginning of their round. They used to work according to the conditions of the weather, travelling around the parish on foot, carrying their tools. The Divisional Surveyor, should he be passing, would know where they were working by the presence of a red flag in the lane.

Nowadays a lengthman has a small van to carry his or her tools in, and a map from the District Surveyor with a list of tasks to be completed and reported on daily, plus paperwork relevant to obtaining an appropriate NVQ qualification. Although we might like to think that yesterday's lengthman was a happy simple soul, he was probably very much beholden to the weather, underpaid for sure, and subject to the whim of every farmer and landowner who wanted snow clearing from his drive in the winter.

Let us see who's performing his tasks now.

Responsibilities for maintenance of green lanes

County Councils are responsible for looking after the existing public rights of way network, which includes green lanes. Highways Departments maintain the surfaces of rights of way.

If vegetation has formed on the highway, it will be the responsibility of the highway authority to clear this. However, under Section 136(1) of the Highways Act 1980, if the surface of a Byway is being damaged because no wind and rain can reach the surface, the highways authority may apply to a magistrates court for an order to be served on the owner or occupier requesting cutting, pruning plashing or lopping to be carried out. Failure to comply within 10 days can lead to a fine.

Overhanging vegetation is usually the responsibility of the landowner. If a tree which overhangs a highway or footway obstructs the passing of vehicles or pedestrians or interferes with sight lines or street lights, the **Highway Authority** may ask the owner or occupier to deal with it. If this does not happen, they may carry out the work and pass on the bill. The same rule applies to diseased or dead trees which are dangerous.

Tree growth may prove a nuisance in green lanes which back on to private property. However there is no requirement in law to keep a private hedge trimmed, nor to prevent trees spreading over a boundary. The tree owner is not obliged to cut back overhanging branches, but the person whose property is overhung has the right to cut back the branches to the boundary in order to remove the nuisance. Just how to do this legally is a matter to discuss with your Local **Planning Authority** tree officer.

Gates and stiles are also the responsibility of the **landowner**, although they can get assistance with maintaining these from the Highways Authority, should they become part of a Parish Paths Partnership maintenance scheme, for example (see Chapter 6, 'How to Get Involved').

Regarding signposting: if not already signposted, Highways Authorities and Parish Councils will be encouraged to work together to signpost an unclassified road, erecting a post with its name at the point where it joins a metalled road. According to Section 27 of the Countryside Act 1968 as amended by Section 65 of the Wildlife and Countryside Act 1981, Highways Authorities have a duty to erect and maintain signs where a BOAT leaves a metalled road.

The Wildlife and Countryside Act 1981

Section 53 of this Act is addressed to Highways Authorities. It outlines the duty which Highways Authorities have to keep a copy of the Definitive Map on view; these may be consulted by the general public. This will show all the highways in the area and questions can be asked as to their status, which is always under review.

Section 54 of the Act states that every RUPP must be reclassified as a BOAT, bridleway or a footpath.

Maintenance of Byways and RUPPs (the legal side)

The Wildlife and Countryside Act of 1981 provides that RUPPs re-classified as BOATs shall be maintainable at public expense. RUPPs themselves are only so maintainable if the way was a public highway on 31st August 1835 (The Highways Act of 1835) or if statutory provision has been made for public maintenance.

The Highways Act 1980 makes it the duty of a highway authority (the County Council or Unitary Authority) to maintain highways which are maintainable at public expense. Government advice (Circular 1/83) is that the standard of maintenance should be sufficient to allow a route to serve the purpose for which it is normally used throughout the year i.e. there is no duty to maintain byways and RUPPs as public roads.

(Extracted from GLEAM [Green Lanes Environmental Action Movement] Newsletter, Autumn 1998).

They may also erect waymarks along the route. The sign must include the status, and at the discretion of the Authority, may indicate the destination and distance of a route. North Lincolnshire County Council have registered some of their UCRs and RUPPs as streets, so as to bring them within their highways budget.

What is important here is that status has to be shown, but destination, distance and additional waymarking along the route are discretionary. Some authorities, by not showing the status of the lane, avoid the problems caused by restricting users. This is where the trouble really begins! So before going any further, let's get down to defining our terms.

HIGHWAYS AND RIGHTS OF WAY

These are two different classes of routes (remember that the term 'green lane' is just a descriptive term and has no legal status). From 1835 onwards, what we call green lanes had become increasingly neglected by Highways Authorities, as the burden of maintaining tarmacked roads increased in proportion to car ownership and use. A survey made in 1976 showed that there were over 150,000 miles of unsurfaced roads, footpaths and bridleways in the UK. As they were at the bottom of the list in terms of priority for maintenance, naturally they became neglected. But now, with an upturn in their use for recreational purposes, it is appropriate that they should be more the concern of Rights of Way Officers than Highway Surveyors.

A Right of Way carries the same definition as a highway, and by convention excludes roads normally used by motor vehicles. Strictly speaking there is a distinction in that a Right is an abstract thing, whereas a highway is a tangible strip of land. There are three different types of rights of way:

A Fable for Today

WHEN A TANGIBLE STRIP OF LAND MET A RIGHT OF WAY

Coming round the corner of Church Path, he was met head-on by an angel. He didn't know which side to take, to dodge to the left or the right, or maybe he should just keep straight on.

"Sorry," the angel murmured.

"Please, no surely". . . he hesitated. "Surely I should apologize, after all this is your right of way."

The angel gently wafted its wings in amusement and then sang out:

"Every spirit's right of way, but your strip of land."

Then he noticed that the angel's feet were in fact levitating.

Public footpaths

Access is allowed on foot only and with an invalid carriage.

Public bridleways

Access is allowed on foot, on horseback, leading a horse, on a bicycle (but cyclists must give way to walkers and people on horseback), an invalid carriage, and possibly an additional right to drive animals.

Byways

Access is 'open to all traffic' although in practice they are often unsuitable for most road vehicles. There is a DETR pamphlet entitled 'Making the Best of Byways' (July 1997), which is a guide concerning public and vehicular rights on unsealed ways (see Bibliography). In addition to this, the DETR lists the following:

> CRF—Public path sometimes shown on definitive maps as 'carriage road used mainly as a footpath' or
> CRB—'carriage road used mainly as a bridleway'.

So those are the Rights of Way—here are the other routes.

Rights of Way

Rights of Way came into being at the time of the Enclosure Acts in the eighteenth century, and were intended to keep such ways open to the public while landowners were busy carving up the countryside to their advantage. Naturally not all landowners thought like this, and did not dedicate their rights of way to the public. Today, after twenty years' use a Right of Way is deemed to be dedicated to the public.

Byways Open to All Traffic (BOATs)

This is a carriageway—i.e. a Right of Way for vehicular traffic—but one which is used mainly for the purpose for which footpaths and bridleways are used, i.e. for walkers and horse riders.

Rights of access on green lanes (as highways) can vary. Green lanes can be any of the above (footpath, bridleway or byway).

The following provide clarification on some routes which are also considered to be green lanes and are not Rights of Way but Highways, by nature of their physical definition:

A *road*—Any length of highway or any other road to which the public have access; includes bridges over which a road passes. The public may access as of right or by permission of the landowner.

A *carriageway*—A way over which the right of way is on foot, on horseback, on pedal cycles, and in or on vehicles (horse-drawn or motorized).

Roads Used as Public Paths (RUPPs)

This is defined as a way for which bridleway rights have already been conclusively proved in law, unless vehicular rights can also be proved to exist upon it. Under the Wildlife and Countryside Act 1981, every RUPP is required to be

---

Duties and Powers of the Highway Authority

Some of their most important statutory duties include:

- protecting the public's right to use and enjoy rights of way;
- maintaining the surface of most rights of way;
- preventing the closure or obstruction of any highway;
- ensuring that farmers comply with the law that paths over cultivated land are properly restored after they have been disturbed and remain apparent on the ground hereafter;
- ensuring that farmers do not allow crops to make the use of any right of way inconvenient;
- ensuring that the legal record of all rights of way, called the 'definitive map and statement', is kept up to date;
- **signposting rights of way from metalled highways and providing additional signs and waymarks where these are necessary along any path.**

The highway authority's discretionary powers allow it to:

- create new paths by agreement with the landowner;
- make orders to create, divert and extinguish rights of way;
- improve rights of way, including the provision of seats and street lighting; and provide footpath wardens.

Vehicular Rights

"Means of transportation running on wheels" have a right to pass and re-pass over a way. The vehicle can be owned publicly or privately (although public transport is actually provided for the public, it is not owned by them). Public vehicular rights are allowed according to what is defined in law as "balance of probabilities" of historical use. How these can be proven relies upon historical evidence such as the documents relating to the Enclosure Acts (see chapter on 'Who Used Green Lanes?'). In the absence of the documents, if continuous public vehicular use can be proven over a period of 20 years prior to 1st December 1930, this is also valid.

reclassified as a BOAT, a bridleway or a footpath. Where it is still shown as a RUPP, the reclassification has not yet been carried out.

According to the Wildlife and Countryside Act of 1981 (Statue 81), a RUPP shall be classified as:

a) A Byway Open to All Traffic, if a public right of way for vehicular (i.e. any kind of wheeled traffic) has ever been shown to have used the path.
b) A Bridleway, if public vehicular rights do not exist and public bridleway rights have not been shown not to exist. (The double negative is in the legislation!)
c) A Footpath, if neither a nor b applies.

There is no provision in the legislation for the suitability for vehicular use of a RUPP, nor for any other amenity consideration to be taken into account when a RUPP is re-classified; if public vehicular rights are shown to exist, it must be re-classified as a byway. The re-classification is generally welcomed by all user groups.

Drove Roads or Driftways
This is a way over which there is the right to drive animals. A carriageway carries the right of driftway, but not vice versa.

Unclassified Roads (UCR)
This is the lowest category of 'public road'. Access is open to all traffic, although in practice the track may be unsuitable for most vehicles. It is a highway maintainable at public expense, other than a way such as an A, B or C road. Further evidence from elsewhere is needed to establish conclusively the existence of vehicular rights. UCRs appear on maps as white roads.

Private lanes with no public rights of access
Most green lanes fit into the first four categories given above, and may be used for public access. There are, of course, private lanes with no public rights of access.

Permissive paths

These are routes over which there is no right of access, but the landowner allows the public to use the route.

Highways

These are best defined in common law as "a way over which all members of the public have the right to pass and re-pass". This use must be as of right, not on sufferance or by licence. May be surfaced or unsurfaced.

CONFLICTS AMONG USERS

Jusserand's *Wayfaring Life in the Middle Ages* gives a vivid description of the dangers of travel in mediæval times. One of the safeguards against attack was to carry a stave with you of six foot or more (called a bullroarer), which you would twirl around your head at the sign of any approaching travellers.

That was certainly a practical way to sort out the problems of conflicting user interests, and one which, in one form or other has probably existed for a long time, but not any more. 'Rights of Way' means just what it says—and those who seek them are many and varied. Just how do they square up against each other?

In English law there are three classes of highway, which can be matched with three classes of user:

1. Footpath   Walker
2. Bridleway   Horse-rider
3. Carriageway   Vehicle

It is the co-existence of these classes and users which leads to complications. Here is a more detailed breakdown of the users.

1. Walkers: both long distance, regular and occasional users.
2. Farmers and other agriculturalists who use green lanes as access roads for their occupations, including forestry.
3. Horse-riders.
4. Horse- and carriage-drivers.
5. Mountain bike riders and ordinary cyclists.
6. Motorcyclists and trial riders.
7. Four-wheel drive vehicles (4WD).
8. Motorized vehicles using access roads for purposes other than occupational, e.g. tanks used in 'war game' routes.

The magazine *Byway and Bridleway*, in its July edition in 1998, argued the case for allowing some long used cycle tracks to be used by horses as well (horse-riders first allowed cyclists to share bridleways with them in 1968).

If things don't work out, then maybe yet another type of highway needs to be named: a cycleway, which would be a right of way for walkers and pedal cyclists only. The amount of legislation piling up around this issue makes one fear that a class of highway dedicated to tandems or tricycles only might appear in time.

So, which combinations of users don't seem to be working?

When walkers and horse-riders meet on a lane, whether it is classified as a footpath or a bridleway, there is rarely conflict. The same can be said for 2, 4 and 5 in the above list.

But what about sharing Rights of Way with motorized vehicles? Conflict is a politically loaded word, so let's just say it is easier to run with those who are self-propelled than with those who are driven by fossil fuels. Historically, one cannot discount the accidents which must have occurred when gigs, barouches and stage coaches came careering round the corner and squeezed a group of market-goers up against a hedge.

As the ownership of 4WDs has increased, so has their participation in off-road driving.

Restricting users by voluntary agreements

LARA (The Motoring Organizations' Land Access and Recreation Association) has its own code of voluntary restraint. This organization is embraced by all the major motoring organizations to address the problem of off-road vehicles, both 4WD and motorbikes. One of the most difficult areas where 'co-existence' has been questioned is on The Ridgeway in Berkshire and Oxfordshire.

Because this organization is admired and respected by the 'off-roaders' who make up its membership and are financially involved by paying subscriptions, they (the members) are far more likely to respond to the idea of 'voluntary restraint' when put forward by LARA, than when such an idea is proposed by a Highway Authority. People's goodwill is much more in evidence when they part with their money on a voluntary basis, rather than when the Highway Authority exacts its dues through taxation and the law; such is human nature.

Voluntary restraint agreements are very simple, and quick to apply. LARA's guidelines for implementing them are as follows.

Is it relevant? Restraint must be likely to solve a real problem.
Is it minimal? It must not extend beyond what is needed. If motorcycles, say, are not a problem, do not include them.
Is it finite? The scheme can extend to three months, extendable for another three if real progress is being made and more time is seen to be needed.
Does it offer no threat even to hidden rights? Clearly it must not be possible to claim later that because users stopped when asked, they were obviously using the lane by permission.
Is the arrangement legal?
Are all relevant users also offering restraint? A problem of general overuse will not be resolved if only vehicle use cases are checked.
Do all local users within LARA agree? Compliance will be limited if users have no 'ownership' of the deal.
Is it user-led? One of the benefits of such a scheme is the publicity, locally and among user groups, which arises from successful co-operative initiatives. This motivates users to obey signs and co-operate elsewhere.
Are there alternative routes? Neighbouring alternatives must be

unobstructed and clearly available. In this regard, a 'secret' UCR is a poor alternative for a signed BOAT.

The voluntary restraint order principles go with LARA's Code of Conduct, which asks vehicle users to pay attention to 'The Four Ws':

Weather Do not travel green roads when they risk being damaged beyond a point of natural recovery when the weather improves.
Weight Do not use lanes which may be seriously damaged by the weight of your vehicle.
Width Do not use lanes which are too narrow for your vehicle.
Winches Use only when unavoidable and take great care not to damage trees, walls etc while recovering.
Remember that wildlife faces many threats and green lanes can be valuable habitats. Take special care in spring and early summer.

AllWheel Drive Club members take part in National Green Lane Day in March, when they work with local authorities to maintain the state of the lanes they use. The Club is also involved in establishing a 'Guardian Lane Scheme', which aims to set up a nationwide list of volunteers who monitor and carry out maintenance work—similar to the 'Adopt a Path' and 'Parish Partnership' schemes.

Areas in Wiltshire, Essex, Berkshire, Oxfordshire, Lake District National Park, Pembrokeshire National Park, Exmoor National Park have all been subject to Voluntary Restraint Orders.

I should point out that LARA is not the only group with volunteer helpers willing to make good their damage: such volunteers also exist within the Long Distance Walkers Fellowship and The Horse Riders' Fellowship. There is also

LARA Voluntary Restraint Sign successfully used on a Byway in Berkshire.

LARA's View on Unsurfaced Routes

Geoff Wilson of LARA says:

"The basic principle being pushed is to create a hierarchy of unsurfaced vehicular routes, i.e. some routes only for certain classes of vehicle (by weight or type), some which will sustain all-weather/all-season use, some which would benefit from more sophisticated types of management and some routes with special historical qualities which could be designated Heritage Byways."

a Code of Conduct for members of the Rough Stuff Fellowship (formerly the Mountain Bike Users Association).

Restricting use by legislation

As has been pointed out, this is when restriction is enforced by an authority which does not necessarily include representation from all users.

Traffic Restriction Orders (TROs)

As opposed to voluntary restraint orders, TROs are more expensive to implement, unpopular and controversial. They cost approximately £3,000 per lane. Legal definitions have to be set out very clearly when local authorities have to enforce a TRO. They work to the DoE Circular 2/93 paragraph 13, which states that TROs may be made to prohibit, restrict or regulate traffic for the following reasons:

1. Preventing danger to persons or other traffic using the road.
2. Preserving the character of the road for use by persons on horseback or foot.
3. Preserving the amenity of the area through which the road runs.

The British Driving Society's View

Mrs J. Dillon, Executive Secretary of the British Driving Society, writes:

"Access to green lanes is so important to people who drive horses and ponies because there is little pleasure in driving on public roads, where we are a nuisance to motorists, and open country is far more difficult with a vehicle behind the horse than it is for a ridden horse. The majority of our members have native ponies, or similar, and a two-wheeled cart which can seat two people. The impact on unmade surfaces is usually less than with a ridden horse, because we move at a more sedate pace, and the cart wheels are narrow with smooth rubber tyres so have less impact than a mountain bicycle. Unfortunately, when we refer to 'horses and carriages', people have a vision of a team of four big horses and a coach!"

However mild this may sound, it could have sweeping consequences, so a TRO must also take into consideration the following: 'The access needs of farmers and residents of property along a byway'. The wording of the TRO must be done in such a way that it only applies to those classes of vehicle which are known to be causing problems.

A TRO may be a temporary or seasonal measure—for example to be implemented in the muddy season, the nesting season, on Sundays only, restricted to weight or width or type of vehicle—or enforced because of maintenance. It may be necessary to monitor whether recreational vehicles or farm vehicles are eroding a lane.

I feel that one very important point has been missed here: the nature of the lane itself. The surfaces are 'unmade', yet are being driven over by vehicles manufactured for 'made' surfaces where all natural life has already been eliminated. It is not a question of 'regulating the ground' (i.e. providing a regular surface), but of preserving it. In the early days of steam-rollers, it was not uncommon to find plaques on bridges which stated that it was not appropriate to cross them with locomotives because the bridge would be destroyed. A bridge is a man-made structure and easily repaired, but a strip of living land is not such a straightforward matter. People can tidy up, but natural regeneration is another matter.

Farmers and landowners

When questioned during the Dartington Institute Study on Green Lanes in 1985, farmers' representatives accepted that the highway authority should repair only the surface of a lane which is a highway of any designation, and

The Lake District

Bob Cartwright, Head of Park Management for the Lake District National Park Authority, has identified 146 routes within the park which are regularly used by 4WD vehicles, sometimes in convoys up to 17 vehicles long:

"It is fundamentally an inappropriate activity for a national park and we have been increasingly concerned about the impact on the landscape and local communities." (Interview with Joanne O'Connor in *The Observer,* 10 Sept 2000)

The Lake District is in terms of geology badly suited to heavy use of any kind, as its soft peaty soil is subject to rutting and waterlogging.

The interview also contained the following statement from Richard Bedall, Chairman of the British Off Road Driving Association:

"I have a lot of sympathy with the national parks, but they are fighting the wrong battle. It's not a question of regulating the ground but regulating the people with some kind of basic training. There are lots of people charging about the countryside in four-wheel drive vehicles who are totally ignorant. You have to have a licence to drive on the road, so why not have one for driving off-road too?"

that the neighbouring farmers should be responsible for the upkeep of any walls or hedges. However, if a lane is a footpath or bridleway, the Council would need to maintain it only for such purposes; the farmer then had to do any additional repairs if he wanted to keep it suitable for his and other farm vehicles. To see whether they understood these dual obligations, the farmers interviewed were asked who was supposed to repair the lanes under survey, and who actually did these repairs. They believed that it was their responsibility where they had caused the damage, but that that the Highways Department had responsibility for general maintenance. The answers did not vary much from area to area, but differed slightly according to the status of the lane.

In the year 2000, farmers and landowners were still critical of the enforcement action being taken by the Highways Authorities, who can compel them to clear these lanes even if they do not cause the damage themselves.

In the Peak District, out of eighteen farmers interviewed for a survey, only three thought they were themselves responsible for repairs; the remainder thought that 'the Council' was liable for repairs . Again, only two said that the Council ever did any repair work; in other cases it was left to the farmer to do what he felt was necessary for his own use of the lane. All those to whom it applied knew that private roads were entirely their own responsibility, even if they were used by the public.

Damage caused by tractors can be minimized by encouraging farmers to use ATVs (All-Terrain Vehicles) whenever possible in lanes, rather than 4WD vehicles or tractors.

It should be remembered that we tend to think of 'recreational' vehicles as being wholly responsible for the churning up of lanes, but this is not always the case, as both forestry and agricultural plant vehicles can achieve the same results. Excessive horse-riding over a bad surface, and using the lane for rough mountain biking, can have the same effect.

One of the costs involved in a TRO might include the erection of bollards or other obstructions to control the traffic. If only 4WD vehicles are to be

Green Lanes not used as Destinations: Essex County Council's Approach

Gerald Gunning, of the Planning Department of Essex County Council, commenting on the Council's Policy concerning green lanes:

"If lanes become destinations instead of contributing to the experience of tranquility enjoyed by those who venture into deepest Essex, their value in the landscape would be soon lost. The point of the policy is to fit traffic to the lanes and not lanes to the traffic to save them from the "improvement" which would be needed if they carried more vehicles. I am sure you will understand this. Anyone celebrating the value of quiet places has this dilemma, and responsibility bears more heavily when the resource is so fragile." (January 1997)

excluded, then a lockable gate must be put up which leaves a gap of 1.15 metres to one side so that horses, walkers, cyclists, motorcyclists can get through. Keys will be issued for those who need to gain access to a dwelling. The barrier does, however, prevent an obstacle to carriage drivers and wheelchair users.

Although costly, the fact that the TRO no longer has to be advertised in the London Gazette has made a saving of £200-£300 on the overall cost.

In the past, local authorities have sometimes proposed TROs on a 'pre-emptive strike' basis: for example, a newly surfaced bridleway may look as if it would deteriorate if vehicles were allowed to use it, and a TRO will stop this from happening.

Extinguishing Rights

By the sound of them, these are even more final than TROs. The authority must prove that the route is 'unnecessary' (see Section 116 of the Highways Act 1980).

Segregation of users

This is often a costly process, but does allow different users to exist side by side in completely different avenues of communication. There are examples of this in the Lake District, where new paths have been created alongside existing rights of way: field paths alongside tarmac roads (see the argument for 'buffer zones' put forward by English Heritage, in Chapter 2).

Green lanes as a distinct category of highway

In 1966 The Council for the Protection of Rural England came up with the idea of classifying green lanes separately from other Rights of Way and Highways, which seemed a valiant attempt to extricate the problem from being one of definition:

> ". . . that should a new category of rights of way be developed which was auto-matically protected from public motorized vehicle use, except for purposes of access to land and property, then they should be called 'Green Lanes' as this is a phrase which already has resonance with the public and which aptly portrays the character of many of these routes."

This new category was based upon the highway's surface, but the CPRE believe that more consideration of wider environmental issues should be made. That was back in 1966, and now the argument for a separate classification is even stronger.

GLEAM (the Green Lanes Environmental Action Movement) is supported by 93 MPs, and the number is rising. It is dedicated to the preservation of green lanes as historically and environmentally important sites. These values cannot be preserved while green lanes are used by fossil-fuel-driven vehicles.

There are other user groups who need to have their say concerning the use of green lanes: wheelchair users, for example, or as the legislation calls them, invalid carriage users.

The problems caused by 4WD users are no greater than those created by people who use lanes as rubbish dumps without actually blocking up the way. There is also the problem of squatters upon 'tracks' (where traditionally they have legally been allowed to stay). When the status of 'tracks' is changed on the new Definitive Map, they may no longer have such squatters' rights.

Although I have covered all the main points of view in this section, the legislation and the individual cases concerning user rights on green lanes is changing all the time, and can only be considered on an individual and local basis and by studying the legal procedures involved.

Maintenance groups

Let us now look at who uses green lanes: irrespective of whether their usage is legal, and whether they are in harmony with their fellow citizens.

The DETR recommends that farmers should be used as contractors to the authority when maintenance work on green lanes is necessary. This would mean that rather than presenting the farmer with a bill for work to be done, they will in fact pay him to perform the work. This has worked successfully in Nottinghamshire, and also in Jersey:

> "With walkers in mind Jersey has developed a network of over 40 miles of 'Green Lanes'. These are signposted, and aim to give precedence over the motor car, with a speed limit of just 15 mph. For an island only 9 miles by 5, Jersey has a profusion of quiet country lanes. The hedgerows and open fields are home to many rare species of flora and fauna."

More examples of this kind of adoption are included in Chapter 6 on 'How to Get Involved'.

Green lanes are increasingly used today. Sometimes they have become part of a national trail or network of rights of way for a particular purpose—for example the Health Walks introduced in Suffolk by Helen Sams, as part of the Stepping Out partnership between the Countryside Agency and several District Councils. There is a Macmillan Way long distance footpath, including

Touring Green Lanes

Mr. Brian Eaton (aged 85), from Stockport in Cheshire, recently undertook a tour which involved green lanes. He stated that his purposes were as follows:

a) To put on record matters relating to some of the old packhorse trails, drovers roads and other historic routes, together with ancient buildings etc., changing customs and environmental issues.
b) To collect donations for PAMSHAPS (People's Acute Medical Services and Horse and Pony Sanctuaries). 100% of all donations will go to the good causes concerned.

Such sponsored events using green lanes are on the increase.

stretches of green lanes. But at least by using them (sensitively) we will not lose them.

In February 1998 there was a public enquiry in Dunstable concerning green lane reclassification. The result of this enquiry as far as two green lanes were concerned was that they had their status changed from RUPPs to BOATs, even though the Town Council had hoped they might become Bridleways rather than Byways. However (and I quote from Mr. Omer Roucoux's helpful correspondence on this case):

"This does not mean that the lanes are 'open to the traffic', but that it is now the responsibility of the Town Council to regulate the circulation. Actually the County Council has placed barriers and signs prohibiting vehicular traffic on most of them. So, in a way the County Council has lost its request, but has obtained the responsibility and the related expenses to control the traffic on these lanes." (4th July 2000)

If the lanes are downgraded to just being bridleways, the owners of the adjoining land may argue that the present width of the lanes is not necessary. They could try to reclaim some of the land, thus making the way much narrower, and destroying a historic feature of the landscape.

Employment opportunities & Greenways

With the creation of new rights of way and their consequent maintenance, new jobs in the countryside will be forthcoming. Such opportunities have been researched by the Countryside Agency, and put together in a scheme known as the Greenways Project.

Tales such as the following (collected by the CPRE) go some way to predicting what will happen in the future to some green lanes which run parallel to minor roads. Will they be opened up to accommodate the growing number of people seeking to avoid motor car congestion?

"Collops Lane, near the small market town of Dunmow in Essex, used to be a place where children played and cycled. Now traffic uses it as a rat run to the A120 and local people say they 'do not feel able to walk the lane with any degree of relaxation or safety'."

The aim is that by establishing Greenways, the rights of all users will be protected:

"Greenways are networks of largely car-free off-road routes, connecting people to facilities and open spaces in and around towns, cities and to the countryside. for shared use by people of all abilities on foot, bike or horseback, for commuting, play or leisure." (Countryside Commission)

This initiative aims to encourage government, the public, businesses and local authorities to redirect finances into walking and cycling, and to encourage communities to call for safe, high quality routes that cater for all needs. The initial study (prompted by fears of gridlock) was made in Hull and East Riding. Greenways fit into the area's overall transport strategy, and contribute towards creating a more sustainable transport system which offers cyclists and walkers a safe, traffic-free journey to work. About half of the households in Hull do not have the use of a car, as compared to a UK average of one-third, so here is an opportunity to keep it that way.

And although there have been extensive road improvements in the city over recent years, traffic flows in the urban area have exceeded forecasts and the existing network is rapidly becoming congested. For these reasons, a balanced transport system is being developed, including public transport, cycling and walking. The city already has many cycleway developments along old railway lines linking town and country, and a Greenway network could make use of these.

This is one of the positive ways forward for green lane users, and can be adopted in other areas to fit in with sustainable transport policies.

> "Our research has shown that traffic on country lanes may increase by an average of over 164% over the next 30 years." (from DoE/DoT Consultation Paper, 'Vehicles on Byways', 1996)

This shows that the use of green lanes is likely to increase, as walkers, cyclists and horse riders find metalled roads increasingly dangerous.

In 1998 the Countryside Commission outlined its proposals for 'Rights of Way in the 21st Century': in essence, they (RoWs) would belong to a sustainable transport network. Objective 7 of their proposal states that there would be distinctions between roads managed for motor traffic and those managed for recreational use. It was proposed that distinctions between utilitarian and recreational travel need to be softened.

People should be encouraged to walk and cycle, and thus use the whole gamut of highways available to them. And yet two years since Objective 7 was published, the phrase 'sustainable transport' is hardly headline news, despite the prospect of ever-diminishing supplies of fossil fuels.

Something to crow about (CROW)

The new Countryside and Rights of Way Bill (CROW), which went through Parliament on 8th December 2000, is a significant document for the future of green lanes. It is hoped that two new pieces of legislation will emerge from it. Firstly, all RUPPs will be designated as restricted byways. This will create a new class of highway which can be traversed on foot, on horseback or leading a horse, and by vehicles which are not mechanically propelled. Secondly, a new way of determining how bridleways were used in the past may be defined. I quote from the most famous case to date, which has previously caused problems in this regard:

> "On 15-17th November 1999 eight motor cyclists were prosecuted by the Crown Prosecution Service at Chesterfield Magistrate's Court for driving on a bridleway (Grimsall Lane, Holmsfield, Derbyshire), but were acquitted. Their alleged offence was driving on a bridleway contrary to Section 34 of the Road Traffic Act 1988 which says '. . . if . . . a person drives a motor vehicle . . . on any . . . footpath or bridleway, he is guilty of an offence.' The defendants admitted that they had ridden their motorcycles on Grimsall Lane.

They were found not guilty because in Section 192 (1) of the same Act 'a bridleway means a way over which the public have the following, but no other, rights of way: a right of way on foot, a right of way on horseback or leading a horse, with or without a right to drive animals of any description along the way. . .' The defence claimed that, because of the words 'but no other' in the definition, the prosecution had to prove that there were no higher rights, i.e. they had to prove that the lane did not carry vehicular rights." (from GLEAM Newsletter, Spring 2000)

Derbyshire County Council, as highway authority, went through all their old records, none of which showed the existence of any rights higher than bridleway rights. However, it could not be said that evidence of vehicular rights could *never* be found. This involves proving a negative, which in this case is effectively impossible.

CROW now states that RUPPs can be re-classified as '**Restricted Byways**'. The definition reads as follows:

(4) "restricted byway rights" means:
a) a right of way on foot,
b) a right of way on horseback or leading a horse and
c) a right of way for vehicles other than mechanically propelled vehicles and

"restricted byway" means a highway over which the public have restricted byway rights, with or without a right to drive animals of any description along the highway, but no other rights of way.
(The Countryside & Rights of Way Act 2000, Ch 37, Part II, Para 48)

Look back at the diagram on page 10. There is one group of roads that still remains vulnerable: UCRs (unclassified roads). Legislation is still needed which will reclassify as Restricted Byways all BOATs and UCRs that are unsurfaced for any part of their length.

Trails

As we have seen, there are many examples of green lanes which form part of an ever-expanding network of national trails. The list is very long already, and there are more planned for the future. Here are just a few:

The Edward Thomas Trail (Oxfordshire and Gloucestershire).
The Severn Way (Worcestershire).
The Pennine Way.
The North Downs Way (from Farnham to Dover in Kent), which is 153 miles (245 km) long.
The Icknield Way, (Bucks, Beds, Herts, Essex, Cambridgeshire, Norfolk and Suffolk), which is 120 miles (190 km) long.
The Cleveland Way (from Helmsley to Filey Brigg), which is 120 miles (190 km) long.
Offa's Dyke Walk, 168 miles (270 km) along the Welsh-English Border.

The Long Distance Walkers Association promote many of these paths, and holds local events all with evocative sounding names:

The Holy Hobble—60 miles (100 km) taking in many churches in the area of Milton Keynes and North Bedfordshire.
The Smuggler's Trod—26 miles (40 km) in North Yorks.
St. Peter's Way Plus—50 miles (80 km) from inland Essex to the coast.

The list grows and grows, from individual societies creating their own routes to leisure attractions expanding their horizons via walking and cycling routes; National Parks and County Councils are also involved in making the country-side more accessible by creating circular and other walks through leaflets and information boards *in situ*.

Finally, there is the European Long Distance Path which runs through Spain, France, Switzerland, Austria, Hungary, Romania, Bulgaria and Greece for 5,000 miles. There must be a few green lanes along the way.

Conclusion

Although this is meant to be a balanced presentation of the requirements of the different user groups, people will still have their own opinions. If you don't wish to become embroiled in the controversy, maybe you should close your eyes to the following paragraphs.

Individual cases will continue to be argued over for years to come, whatever the new legislation dictates. Suffice it to say that, after many years of neglect, green lanes are gradually being brought back into the highway network. They are being incorporated into sustainable and integrated transport systems, whilst retaining their individual character.

On a raw November morning, I stood by the side of a 4WD-frequented green lane, with cars, drivers and spectators all steaming and roaring. Despite the obvious excitement of the event, it was clear to me that green lanes are more appropriate for the nurturing of plants and wildlife than for worshipping of the power of man's mechanical inventions and love of speed. The words of Laurence Binyon, the First World War poet, came into my head. In his poem called 'Fetching the Wounded', an ambulance driver swerves off the road; and look what he discovers:

And swerving leftwards upon noiseless tires
We glide over the grass that smells of dew.
A wave of wonder bathes my body through!
For there in the headlamp's gloom
Tall flowers spring before us like a dream,
Each luminous little green leaf intimate
And motionless, distinct and delicate
With powdery white bloom fresh upon the stem,
As if that clear beam had created them
Out of the darkness.

Nature will speak louder than man, and eventually will lead him back to the roads—where his vehicles belong. In the meantime, given the problems of impending fuel shortages and increasing CO_2 emissions, we should adopt the role of foot-soldiers in the battle for green lanes.

Just as at the moment we find ourselves discussing the right to roam, perhaps we need to remind ourselves of just how successful public access laws have been in some European countries, where different users' rights seem to be co-existing in harmony. Norway, Sweden, Denmark and Germany all offer the public freedom to wander in all uncultivated countryside, forests and coastal areas. They also have walking and cycling rights on farm tracks.

Surely we can achieve this in the United Kingdom as well.

Chapter Six

HOW TO GET INVOLVED

Surveying and recording of green lanes

Bernardette Hardern reports from Tarporley, Cheshire:

"You may be Interested to know of a middle distance Bridlepath which has taken 11 years in the making to achieve, which Cheshire CC finally got going, which I named The Bishop Bennet Way. He was a real person, born 1745 died 1820. Both he and his friend, a Rev Thomas Lemon, worked on this Way. Rev Lemon's favourite hobby was the surveying and recording of old Roman roads throughout England, including parts of Cheshire but mainly in SW England, i.e. Devon and Cornwall, and also in Leicestershire. It must have been a lovely hobby as the countryside was more accessible than it is today."

As we have seen, this idea of the countryside being more accessible has a certain truth in it, given all the various categories of green lane which we have seen registered in the past chapters, and the many different users clamouring to get into them.

There are two kinds of green lanes users who get involved in looking after them. There are those described by Bernardette Hardern (see above), who wish to find out more about the history of the lane, where it once ran, and why. Then there are those who want to get stuck in and help with their upkeep.

For the latter, the Parish Paths Partnership scheme (known as the 3Ps) is just right. For the former (and for local history groups, and individuals foraging in Records Offices), there is the Parish Map scheme.

The Parish Paths Partnership

This is one of the established schemes which will help you with recording your green lanes. They are run by the Highways Authority of your District Council. Grants are given on a parish basis: they are meant to cover the surveying of the rights of way, their maintenance (as described below), the organization of events and publicity to promote the use of the footpath network. Grants are given to volunteers (who can then sub-contract if necessary) to complete these works; they are based on the mileage of RoWs within a parish, any special projects involved (i.e. the construction and fitting of a footbridge), and the administrative costs involved.

Such a grant will enable you to buy in extra help if required, such as that available from the weekly workout teams of BTCV (British Trust for

The Devon Shovel

"The traditional Devon shovel, with the heart-shaped blade and curved handle, is seldom seen in use today because of the increase in mechanical tools. For centuries past it was the one hand tool used as much as any other. Its versatility in dealing with soil, or like materials, such as for lifting, cutting, mixing, scraping and 'spurting' was unequal.

No doubt its origin was with primitive man when he first found he needed to move soil, so he shaped a wooden tool from a piece of split tree trunk with a point for penetration and a wide base for carrying.

With the coming of iron 2,000 years ago a much sharper and more efficient tool was possible. Then the shovel would have realized its full potential, with the development of agriculture on a field scale. One of its prime functions was in the building and maintaining the thousands of miles of Devon turn hedges—all hand built." (by Hubert Snowden, from *Dartington Rural Archives Magazine*)

Conservation Volunteers) available throughout the country. The Parish Paths Partnership now operates in 15 counties—is yours one of them?

All those who get involved in restoring and looking after a lane learn new skills, sometimes using old techniques—scythes as well as strimmers are used. They might get to drive a dumpy truck and roll finings or scalpings to their heart's content. As the happy band of workers marches off into the sunset, one can almost hear the lane expressing its thanks for what has been done to preserve it.

But before you charge in with your bow saws and secateurs, there are many people to inform, as your local Rights of Way Officer will tell you. For example here is a list of those to whom you must write:

1. To the residents' newsletter.
2. To residents directly affected.
3. To the local County Councillor.
4. To the Parish Council.
5. To the District Council.
6. To landowners directly affected.
7. To the Highways Authority.

The letter should contain a description of the objective of the work to be undertaken and the nature of the work; it should say by whom it will be carried out, and how long it is likely to take. It should include the parish, number and grid reference of the route involved.

The areas which your group will work on when looking after the green lane relate to the hedgerow and its trees, the lane's surface, its drainage and the stiles, gates and signposting along its length.

Trees and green lanes

If you think you have a particularly unusual or fine specimen of a tree in your green lane, then you should apply for a Tree Preservation Order. The rule is that if its removal would have a significant impact on the amenity of the area, you should apply for one. The tree will then be protected against felling, pruning or uprooting without the consent of the Local Planning Authority. The order refers to the whole tree including its roots (see also Chapter 4 on Ecology).

It is interesting to note here that according to law, unless their state causes a nuisance, there is no requirement either to keep hedges trimmed or to prevent trees from spreading over a boundary.

If a tree is hanging over a footway and obstructing the passage of pedestrians, it is up to the owner to deal with this. If he doesn't, then the Highway Authority may do so and bill the owner accordingly. Sensible clipping of dangerous branches is always much appreciated by lane users, especially horse riders.

Hedgerow maintenance

Hedges grow from two inches to two feet a year. In order to produce a stock-proof fence—one which is a safe nesting site for birds and which encourages a diversity of plant and tree species, or conversely maintains just one species beautifully (such as beech hedges)—there are just six rules to follow.

1. You do not have to cut your hedge every year.
2. If you produce a rolling pattern of maintenance, a two or three year rotation should work. Hedgerow trees and shrubs only produce flowers, nuts and berries on year-old twigs.
3. Tops need to be cut every two or three years, sides every year.
4. Plant saplings at 50-metre intervals.
5. Cut as late as possible, preferably during January or February.
6. Never cut during the bird breeding season (April to July).

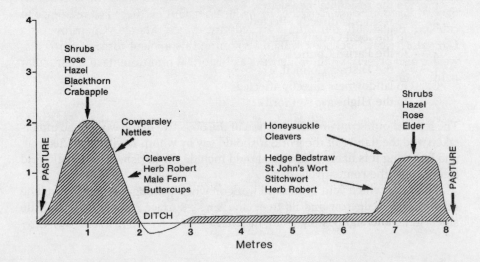

The Man in the Moon

"We are enlightened by a thirteenth-century poem, 'The Man in the Moon', as interpreted by R.J. Menner. The mediæval thoughts of the Man in the Moon as a stupid hedger (like Shakespeare's Moonshine, 'with lanthorn, dog and bush of thorn'), the poem talks of how stupid it would be just to build a hedge from thorns—biodiversity has a long history." (After Rackham, *A History of the Countryside*, Dent, 1986).

Clearance can be undertaken with hand tools or with power tools such as strimmers and brush cutters—the workers can decide which is used.

The ancient art of hedge-laying is both compelling and fascinating; it is also hard and dangerous work. The farm labourers who were able to complete a 30-yard stretch in a day must have been very strong and fit. Volunteers working in teams can achieve these results, and be very proud when they do so.

Drainage and surfaces

This includes the general clearing of vegetation which grows up too thickly within a lane: impenetrable brambles, clumps of stroyle grass, nettles and gorse. When these are removed, there is a general improvement in the drainage of the lane. Creating buddles and drainage channels, and putting in pipes, are all tasks which greatly improve the condition of a lane.

Volunteers can get involved in spreading barrow-loads of scalpings, fines and road burnings to absorb the moisture in very wet passages in lanes.

Cobbled ways

Where there is evidence of cobbles in a lane, there is always a case for re-instating them, and indeed laying extra lengths of cobbles. In *Trackway to Turnpike: the Old Roads of South Herefordshire* by Heather Hurley, there is a reference to cobbled roads still remaining at Ledbury, Much Marcle, Chepstow, and Llangatoch near Crickhowell. By maintaining this ancient form of surfacing, we are also preserving the routeways as historical monuments at a particular point in time.

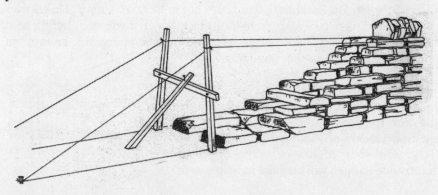

Stone walling

We must no longer think of this as a dying art. There are many newly qualified young stone-wallers in the country who can be sub-contracted by Parish
Councils to repair and build stretches of stone wall appropriate to the area of
the green lane. There are great differences in style between the walls found in
the Peak District, the Yorkshire Moors, Dartmoor or Bodmin Moor.

Creating a new lane

When it is thought appropriate to create a new lane, the banking up of turf
and the planting of saplings can be carried out easily by volunteers, including children. The best way to plant up is to place two offset rows of shrubs
or trees on a bank or along the border of a field or woodland edge, so that
your hedge becomes the one needed to create a lane as well. The saplings,
which should be two years old, should be well watered in, and flanked with
stock-proof fencing to keep off rabbits and deer especially. Tie strips of
sacking or plastic to them to keep them safe from being flailed in the future.
The species you choose must be based on those already growing in your
local hedgerows.

Annual seed collecting event

This occurs on a national scale and is known as Seed Gathering Sunday
(usually the second weekend in October). All you need do is gather a group of
friends or volunteers (from your Parish Paths Partnership scheme, for
example) and set off with your collecting bags. You can then plant the seeds in
root trainers and sit back and wait for results.

However, tree planting schemes are not the complete answer to the
problem, as Dr. Oliver Rackham pointed out in the Spring 2000 edition of *Tree
Warden News*:

> "Money creates the idea that trees that have grown by themselves and cost
> nothing are valueless. People promote trees that they have paid for, and liqui-
> date those they have not paid for."

This is of course far less likely to happen in a lane where the value of long-
standing individual trees and a well managed hedgerow speak for themselves,
but nevertheless Dr. Rackham's words are not to be taken lightly. He encourages tree planting to take place from local stock, which involves collecting seed
at a local level. A good opportunity to do this would be to organize an event in
your area on Seed Gathering Sunday.

Gates and stiles

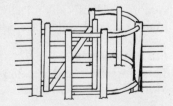

Under the 3Ps partnership, landowners are eli-
gible for free gates and stiles within their
schemes. Leaders of volunteer groups such as
BTCV, and your Rights of Way Officer or
Countryside Ranger, will be there to help you fit

Green Lane Factfile

The South Hams has 191 individual green lanes.

There are around 750km (450 miles) of paths of which 300km (180 miles) run along green lanes.

Many have been forgotten and have fallen into disrepair.

It costs up to £10,000 to repair a badly storm damaged lane.

It costs around £200 per kilometre to maintain a green lane.

Replacing a stile with a kissing gate to improve access for the less mobile costs around £200.

Locals, businesses and visitors to the area can help with these costs by donating part of transport costs, ticket sales, accommodation, the cost of food and drink to the scheme. South Hams District Council is willing to provide help for others interested in knowing how the scheme works: please contact The Green Tourism Officer, SHDC, Follaton House, Plymouth Road, Totnes, Devon TQ9 5NE. Tel: 01803 861297, su.beswick@south-hams-dc.gov.uk.

them. Small footbridges can also be constructed off-site and delivered to difficult areas along a green lane.

Other schemes to promote the conservation of lanes

Grants are available from MAFF under the Countryside Stewardship Scheme. Hedge restoration, which includes hedge-laying, hedge-coppicing and hedge-planting, will be given a grant of £3 per metre.

The Farming and Wildlife Advisory Group within your County Council can give an annual grant (administered through the Countryside Stewardship Scheme) towards the creation of field margins: up to £538 per year can be paid for keeping verges on the field side of hedgerows (and lanes) as wildlife buffer zones. These link one habitat to another and allow wild creatures to enter or remain where they are.

Payback schemes related to Green Tourism

As part of a new green tourism scheme in the South Hams of Devon, a unique green lanes improvement project has been funded through a partnership between visitors, business and the community. This could be a blueprint for other authorities. 'On the Right Tracks' is a programme aimed at opening up and conserving these historic Green Lanes and footpaths for the enjoyment of visitors and locals alike. The work is costly, but even the smallest donation can make a big difference (see box above).

Future Forests

This Somerset- and London-based organization, founded in 1995 by Dan Morrell and Sue Welland, seeks to intervene at governmental level in the

Making the Best Choices

"A farmer walking across a field was questioned by an ecologist. The ecologist asked him if he cared about the future of the planet, about the earth which he tended and was in his care. The farmer replied wisely by questioning his questioner:

"Do you wear a pair of boots two sizes too small when you go walking or do you wear the right size ones?"

The ecologist replied that obviously he wore the right size ones.

"And so do I, my friend," said the farmer. "But sometimes I have to wear wellington boots—I have to protect myself against the environment."

The ecologist was puzzled and said that surely shoes or wellington boots made no difference to the environment.

"Exactly," said the farmer. "But choosing the right equipment for the job makes a lot of difference to the user."

A car whizzed along the open road in the distance. The ecologist thought:

"He's right. Whichever way we choose to travel, the effect on the environment will be the same. It is we the travellers who must make the best, the wisest choices. But in the future we must make the best choices for our planet first, and ourselves last."

—from *The Book for Those Who Travelled Hopefully and Never Arrived*

debate about carbon dioxide emissions and to give individuals and corporations an immediate solution: to plant the appropriate number of trees to offset their carbon emissions. Although not always appropriate in the maintenance of a green lane, there are times when the scheme could be used—for example when a new planting scheme is appropriate to fill a gappy hedge.

In ecological and historical terms, CO_2 is a great destroyer of the green lanes environment, and planting trees to offset this could be an answer. Contact Future Forests (see Appendix I) to find out whether it is appropriate for your group to take part in the scheme.

The Long Distance Walkers Association

There are many local branches of walking groups organized by The Ramblers and The National Trust, and there are also guided walks programmes run by many district and local councils, national and wildlife parks. All will take you through green lanes at some point, but if you want green lane coverage on a grander scale, then the LDWA will be of interest to you. It was founded in 1972, when its membership was just 355; today it is over 7000. It publishes its own handbook of trails and path charts, and a journal (*Strider*). Each local group has insurance for path clearance activities, and many of the individual members are involved with the Councils, Trusts and Associations who work to improve the footpath network. The Association defines a LDW as an extended walk in a rural area, especially one that exceeds twenty miles in length (see Bibliography for contact details).

The Woodland Trust

The Woodland Trust is the UK's leading charity dedicated solely to the protection of our native woodland heritage. Founded in 1972, it has grown into an organization which protects national and internationally important sites. All have public access, and many have green lanes adjacent to them, leading through them or to them (see Chapter 3, 'Every Lane has its History'). They have created 2,000 hectares of new native woodland, and have a target of creating a total of 3,000 hectares by 2003. Their volunteer programme includes work in woodlands, tree planting and access lanes (see Appendix VII for contact details).

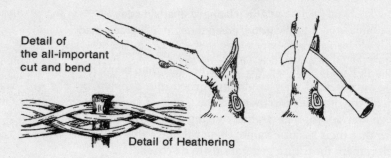

Detail of the all-important cut and bend

Detail of Heathering

Educational involvement

Many volunteer programmes have provision for children to come along and help. The best way to involve children is on the practical level first. Over the years I have developed educational material for primary and secondary children, including a play called 'The Lost Lane' and activity sheets, some of which is available for you to download from our website (see Appendix VII).

Beating the Bounds

These ceremonies have recently been revived in many areas, both rural and urban; they provide excellent opportunities for studying green lanes on the ground, on maps and through the medium of written descriptions of the perambulation. The Common Ground scheme whereby local people create their own Parish Map, often includes the recording and depiction of green lanes.

Conclusions

Whatever happens in regard to the future of green lanes and who uses them, let us all bear in mind the fable of the man crossing the field (see box on page 91), which illustrates the basic dilemma which we all face concerning the future of mobility on our planet. We are faced with large scale problems such as population growth, and also with problems at a local level such as the respecting of boundaries, accepting other people's forms of transport and their leisure interests, and the need to travel to gain our livelihoods.

Although I have been involved for over fifteen years in studying, recording and protecting green lanes, I have throughout this period felt that protecting these 'lines in the landscape' which in recent years have been so little used, has an element of antiquarianism about it.

Yet the fact that green lanes have sometimes been classified as Highways must mean that their continuing use is inextricably linked with the future of all roads, not only in the UK but in Europe and the rest of the world. The question of the degree to which we can continue to travel around the planet remains unanswered, and I hope that this book will not encourage us to step back and feel smug about what has been achieved so far.

We should not feel content to leave things as Andrew Marvell describes:

> "Annihilating all that's made
> into a green thought in a green shade."

Green lanes are ancient routes: in fact, they are Green Lanes Used Throughout History (GRUTHs). Today, we see that rather than being *routes* through which people once passed, they are being turned into *destinations*. The only way to retain all the qualities discussed in the Circle of Definition in Chapter One is to keep the appropriate traffic moving through them. This approach will ensure that their historic value, their wildlife value and their value as routes will all remain for future generations to discover.

Appendix I
SURVEY FORMS

Survey form for green lane as recommended by the DETR

○ **Name of parish**

○ **Name of RUPP / BOAT / UCR**

○ **1:10,000 OS grid reference**

○ **Details of owners / occupiers**

○ **Length of route** (km or m)

○ **Width of route** (m)
- Width of narrow sections (m)
- Usable width

○ **Extent and type of waymarking**

○ **Length and condition of each type of surface:-**
- hardcore / gravel (m)
- other rock / riverbed / sand (m)
- grass / earth
  (clay, sand, chalk, peat, etc) (m)
- other (specify) (m)

○ **Gradients (flat, moderate or steep)**

○ **Evidence of use and frequency of use (in broad terms) by:-**
- farm animals
- tractors and other agricultural vehicles
- cars
- four wheel drive recreational vehicles
- motorcycles
- horse drawn carriages
- horses
- bicycles
- walkers
- other traffic

○ **Details and location of problems:-**
- locked / narrow gates
- fences
- cultivation
- vegetation
- other

○ **Estimate of remedial work required:-**
- total length of surface vegetation to be cleared
- total length of overhead vegetation to be cleared
- total length of ditches to be cleared
- total length of surface affected by ruts
- total length of surface affected by deep mud
- other problems

○ **Remedial work requires:-**
- excavator
- chainsaw
- brush cutter
- drainage material
- surfacing material

○ **Number of signposts and waymarks required**

○ **Historical information**

○ **Ecological information**

Source:
Hampshire County Council and Entec UK Ltd

Information required to define a problem (DETR)

○ Acknowledged public status of route - RUPP, BOAT, UCR, Bridleway, Footpath

○ Private access rights

○ Possible 'wrong' recording of status or a need to reclassify

○ Location and importance in network for each class of user

○ Past, present, possible future use

○ History

○ Geology

○ Archaeological and / or ecological significance

○ Record of previous complaints, including instances of nuisance or annoyance

○ Previous remedial measures carried out, including maintenance

○ Condition of route

HEDGEROW SURVEY FORM

Trees and woody shrubs in 30 paces:
Left side:
Right side:
Evidence of bird and animal life:

Trees	Beg L	Beg R	End L	End R
Ash				
Beech				
Birch				
Blackthorn				
Elder				
Elm				
Field Maple				
Gorse				
Hawthorn				
Hazel				
Holly				
Oak				
Privet				
Rose				
Rowan				
Sycamore				

Trees	Beg L	Beg R	End L	End R
Black Spleenwort				
Bracken				
Broad Buckler				
Hard Fern				
Harts Tongue				
Lady Fern				
Maidenhair				
Spleenwort				
Male Fern				
Polypodium				
Soft Shield				

Trees	Beg L	Beg R	End L	End R
Alexanders Arum				
Bedstraw				
Black Bryony				
Bluebell				
Bramble				
Campion				
Celandine				
Cleavers				
Cow Parsley				
Cranesbill				
Dandelion				
Dock				
Foxglove				
Ground Ivy				
Herb Robert				
Hogweed				

Trees	Beg L	Beg R	End L	End R
Honeysuckle				
Ivy				
Knapweed				
Navelwort				
Nettle				
Plantain				
Primrose				
Speedwell				
Stitchwort				
Thistle				
Vetch				
Violet				
Yarrow				
Yellow Toadflax				
Willowherb				
Woundwort				

HISTORICAL INFORMATION

O.S. Sheet: _____ Grid Ref: _____ Parish: _____
Local name: _____ Official status: _____ Dist: _____
Vantage points to: _____
Historical / Archaeological feature observed: _____
Site: _____ Grid Ref: _____ Sketch / Photo: _____
Place name evidence: _____ Evidence of dating from hedgerows & banks: _____
Evidence of lane being part of an ancient system of communication: _____

P3 CONDITION SURVEY

PARISH PATHS *partnership*
A COUNTRYSIDE COMMISSION INITIATIVE

1 Parish: Much Doing	2 Status: Footpath - ~~Bridleway - Byway - BOAT~~ (delete)	3 No.: 10 — 4 Length: 360 (metres)
5 Name of Surveyor: Andy Mann	6 Tel. No.: 01392-382550	7 Survey Date: 10.4.97
8 Starting Point: Fairley Cross		

9 General Condition: Good ☐ — Acceptable ☐ — Usable with difficulty ☑ — Unusable ☐

(EXAMPLE watermark)

10 Grid Reference	11 Structures (Signpost - Stile - Gate - Kissing Gate - Culvert - Sleeper Bridge - Footbridge - Walkway - Steps)	12 Condition O.K.	12 Condition Needs Attention	13 Problems, Obstructions, Projects (General comments overleaf please)	14 Priority This Year	14 Priority Monitor	15 Regular Attention	16 Owner (See 19)	17 DCC Help?
76243870	Signpost		✓	Loose arm		✓		A	
	Stile		✓	Barbed wire across stile	✓			A	
76253870				"Private-Keep Out" sign	✓			A	
				Ploughed – not re-instated	✓			A	
76333868	Bridge 5m		✓	Abutments undercut	✓		Follow up with annual reminder	A,B.	
76353867				Deep holes on path surface	✓			B	
76433842	Kissing Gate	✓						B.C.	✓
76463840				Line unmarked on heathland	✓	✓	Annual strim on line of path.	C	
76923855	Gate		✓	Awkward catch	✓			C	
	Signpost	✓				✓		C	✓

18 Signs — Total number of signposts: 2

Waymarking: Needs Attention ☑ — O.K. ☐

19 Names of owners / occupiers	Address	Tel. No.
A	B. Caffle	Serly Manor, Much Doing.	01392-382000
B	Mr. Abbot	Borough Farm, Much Doing.	01392-383240
C	Mr. Rea	Wytch Farm, Much Doing.	01392-382979
D			

20 Is this route suitable for those with limited mobility? Yes, possibly, would like more advice.

Appendix II
SOME IMPORTANT GREEN LANES, BY COUNTY

In researching *The Green Lanes of England* I contacted all the County Surveyors in England who gave me details of their 'star' green lanes. This has been updated according to any new information received.

BEDFORDSHIRE
The county provided information on the following periods:

Prehistoric
1. The Ridgeway from SP964448-TL003502. Forty Foot Lane from SP932596-SP980627 (part of this is a footpath only).
2. The Icknield Way. From TL085265-TL135301. This section is a green lane.
3. The Theed Way. This originally ran from Linslade in the west, and is still a green lane from TL008264-TL035259 and over the final section TL080265-TL085265, linking in with the Icknield Way at the latter point, as was the intention in prehistoric times.

Roman
Hassell's Hedge, from TL184493-TL198541, part of the Sandy to Godmanchester Roman road.

Anglo-Saxon
Yelnow Lane, from SP954597-SP977594. This could be Prehistoric or Anglo-Saxon.

Mediæval
Sweetbriar Lane TL129466-TL138445.
Green Lane TL226423-TL253418.
Totternhoe group of lanes around TL008214.

CAMBRIDGESHIRE
Although no information was received from the county, a study of its green lanes was made by Ruth Matthias in 1993, entitled *A Strategy for the Management and Protection of Green Lanes in Cambridgeshire* (unpublished diploma dissertation, Birkbeck College, London).

CHESHIRE
Information from the Public Rights of Way Unit stated that a quarter of the lanes in the county have been, or are being, reclassified. Examples of what they

considered to be their best included the following (check with Cheshire ROW to confirm their present status).

Drovers' route

This is a salter's way running from Bank Lane at Jenkin's Chapel; an unclassified county road with a traffic regulation order on the central section. SJ972765 at the Cross to 984766 at the Church (Macclesfield and Alderley Edge).

Lambert's Lane, Congleton. First recorded in 1442. Now classified as Bridleway no. 1.

Parliamentary Enclosure Roads

In February 1997 this RUPP (number 19) was undergoing a change in status. It was proposed that it became a Byway (check with the Department). One is to be found at Tushingham-cum-Grindley, and was set out in an Enclosure Award of 1795.

CLEVELAND (Hartlepool Borough Council)

Roman

Hutton Lane (NZ60601438-NZ60601404).

Mediæval

Gratham to Cowpen Bewley (NZ4827-4825).

In the district of Langbaurgh:

1. In the parish of Guisborough, Ruthergate Road (NZ60101550-NZ60401410).
2. In the parish of Guisborough, Godfalter Hill (NZ54481633).
3. In the parish of Skelton, Airyhill (NZ64901650-NZ72601930).

Drovers' route

Birk Brow to Commondale (NZ6598-1297).

CORNWALL

The counties of Cornwall, Dorset and Devon were not approached for specific green lanes information in the course of writing this book, in order to avoid giving the book too much of a West Country bias. It is generally known that this area of the country is rich in not-too-difficult-to-find green lanes. A Manpower Services Commission Green Lanes Project operated in East Cornwall in the 1980s, and a report on this should be available from the County Council. A book (by Liz Luck—see Bibliography) was also produced.

CUMBRIA

The Sites and Monuments Records office stated that they list drove roads, Roman roads etc., but they cannot check whether or not they fall into the category of green lanes or are in use as paved highways. They were kind enough to issue me with lists which give this information but are too long to be printed out here. Here are some of the definitions given for roads of historical importance: "holloways, trackways, roads, Enclosure roads (dating from pre-

Parliamentary Enclosure times as well), Drove roads, Roman roads, Corpse roads, Coal roads and Turnpike roads".

In the Kirby Lonsdale area along the Fellfoot road (SD635811-SD637785), the artist Andy Goldsworthy has restored some sheepfolds adjacent to where some green drover's lanes run.

DERBYSHIRE

The packhorse routes in the upland part of the county are important. The most obvious route of this type which springs to mind is Doctors Gate, the reputed Roman road between Hope on the Sheffield side of the Pennine Hills over to Glossop on the western side (approximate grid ref. 171854-061947).

Drovers' route

The saltway through Longdendale (030977-156001), which was part of an ancient salters' route from Northwich in Cheshire eastwards over the Pennines. There appear to be 'green lane' sections of this which have been bypassed by the modern road.

Specific material relating to green lanes in the High Peak area of Derbyshire is available in the Dartington Institute Study, which stated that there are over a hundred lanes, amounting to over 150 miles (240 km).

DEVON

See note under Cornwall. This area of the country is rich in green lanes that are fairly easy to find. In the South Hams area alone, the Dartington Institute Study recorded that there are over 500 lanes amounting to over 300 miles (480 km).

The whole of the county was surveyed for green lanes in the 1980s during the course of the MSC Green Lanes Project. Detailed records of this, as well as a report, are available from Devon County Council. See also page 90.

DORSET

See note under Cornwall. Like Devon and Cornwall, this area of the country has many green lanes. In West Dorset alone the Dart Institute study recorded that there are over 600 green lanes amounting to nearly 400 miles (640 km). It is best to apply directly to the Rights of Way department for details of lanes in any specific area.

DURHAM

This county has published many walks leaflets through its Environment Department, and inevitably there will be some stretches of green lane contained in individual walks. The Rights of Way department pointed out lead-mining trails which belong to the mediæval and industrial archæology periods.

ESSEX

I have quoted from a letter (see page 77) which explains their reluctance to point out any specific lanes. Given the threatened status of this county, because of its proximity to London, this attitude is thoroughly understandable.

GLOUCESTERSHIRE

This county publishes its own *Public Rights of Way and Conservation* Magazine which contains information on trails, such as the Gloucestershire Way, and ROWs which contain stretches of green lane.

HAMPSHIRE

The Planning Department of this county issues an excellent publication entitled *Ancient Lanes and Trackways*, many of which are green lanes. They also provided information on green lanes from various historical periods. A paper on the sunken lanes of East Hampshire has recently been written by Mr. J. Ockendon of East Hampshire District Council.

Prehistoric

The Harroway, parts of which run through Hampshire and once ran from Marazion in Cornwall to Dover via Salisbury Plain.
The South Downs Ridgeway between Kimbridge and Lomer and the South Hampshire Ridgeway.
The North Downs Trackway (Pilgrim's Way). This trackway consists of a ridgeway and lower terrace way. The term Pilgrim's Way has been attributed to the higher ridgeway, but really it should be included in this period as Canterbury Pilgrims used it well after its foundation years. There are also other green lanes which belong to this period, running as connectors between the Harroway and the South Downs Way.

Anglo-Saxon

The Cloven Way is supposedly the route taken by Cerdic and Cynric in the late fifth and early sixth centuries. The alignment runs between North and South Charford.
The Lunway, which is described as a true ridgeway. It begins in the old Saxon region west of the River Test, coming from Old Sarum by way of Lobscombe Corner. It reaches the Winchester to Basingstoke road at the Lunways Inn and is joined by a Saxon drove road from Andover to Alresford.

Mediæval

Part of The Old Way: Walbury Camp to Basingstoke (SU559550-564545).

Drovers' route

The Ox Drove (SU414589-428576).

National Trail

On The Isle of Wight a study was made in 1992 with the following title: *A site assessment and management plan for the Tennyson Trail Green Lane and Track on the Isle of Wight.*

HEREFORD AND WORCESTER

This is a region which contains a large number of green lanes and therefore, as with the West Country, further examples are not given here.

KENT

The council provided me with a plethora of information and pointed out that a list of the 'better' lanes which I required could run to over 5000 miles (8000 km). I am listing below examples which show the detail included in their region-by-region Rural Lanes Studies. They issue a booklet which gives details of the trails and walks throughout the county.

Prehistoric

The 'Greenway' follows the foot of the Downs, following roads through Lenham and Charing Heath and on to Brabourne Lees and Stanford.

There are a number of ridgeways used by the Romans when they built their Roman roads, such as the road from Shore to Allhallows on the Hoo Peninsula.

Roman

Richborough to Dover and Canterbury to Benenden in the Weald are green lanes.

LANCASHIRE

The Pennine and Packhorse Trails Trust, based in Todmorden, is seeking to protect as many of these routes as possible. One of the ways in which they are doing this is by producing historical evidence to prove continuing usage of a lane. Their work is invaluable in that it makes people aware of our highway heritage and actively encourages them to save green lanes for future generations to enjoy as BOATs, wherever this is appropriate. The Trust also gave information on the existence of many green lanes in areas such as Calderdale, where lanes led from the industrial valleys up to the farming areas on higher ground.

LEICESTERSHIRE

Prehistoric

Salt Street and Roe House Lane. This runs from Norton Juxta Twycross (431300-306940) for two miles (3 km) to No Man's Heath in Warwickshire (429040-308810).

The Drift and Sewestern Lane. From Harston (484800-332120) for nine miles (15 km) along the boundary between Leicestershire and Lincolnshire to Thistleton (490240-318510).

Roman

Gartree Road forms part of the route from Leicester to Huntingdon, Cambridge and, eventually, Colchester. Burton Overy section from 467650-299480 for one mile to 469060-298690. Shangton to Glooston section from

471740-297160 for 1¾ miles (2.8 km) to 474240-295780.
Part of the Fosse Way from Lincoln to Axmouth. From Stoney Bridge, Sapcote (450370-293000) for three miles (5 km) to High Cross (Venonis), at junction with Watling Street (447240-288700).

Mediæval
Covert Lane and Coplow Lane.
From Scraptoft (464750-305520) via deserted mediæval village of Ingarsby, for four miles (6 km) to Billesdon Coplow (470680-304880).

LINCOLNSHIRE
A study of the green lanes in this county was made in September 1990, entitled *Lincolnshire Green Lanes Project Report: September 1990.* North Lincolnshire has classified many of its green lanes as 'streets'. A particularly interesting group of Turbury paths exists in the Isle of Axholme area.

Prehistoric
See The Drift and Sewstern Lane under Leicestershire.

LONDON
The London Walking Forum is involved in creating green walks round the city. The London Loop includes stretches of green lane within its 72-mile (115 km) circuit, passing through many counties as well as Greater London. The circuit is divided into twenty-three sections. The Thames Path also includes green lanes within its length.

NORTHAMPTON
The council provided me with information which in a few years' time could be expanded upon, once their computerized mapping system is in place. In addition, Northampton Leisure Services have a leaflet entitled *Roads and Trackways through the Ages,* a comprehensive survey which includes a map showing historic routes throughout the county.

Roman
A green lane at Crick runs parallel with the M1 in places.

Anglo-Saxon
A county and parish boundary which runs from the River Trent at Syerston (SK731492-SK795408) to the north-west of Bottesford was identified as being particularly important.

RUTLAND
Now once more a county in its own right, the following information came from the Libraries and Museums department.

Drovers' route
The most important one is Sewestern Lane, which starts in Rutland and stretches northwards into Lincolnshire. It is only green in parts.

Turnpikes

Some references to green lanes within the county are contained within *Turnpikes and Royal Mail of Rutland* (see Bibliography under letter 'R').

SHROPSHIRE

Drovers' route

The Kerry Ridgeway is a track which is reputed to have prehistoric origins but was also a drove road in the 18th and 19th centuries. It starts at Radnorshire Gate near Dalfor and crosses the Kerry Hills to Bishop's Castle. It is either a BOAT or a surfaced highway throughout this distance and is remarkable for its excellent views both northwards and southwards.

The Portway is a track which was certainly in use by drovers and others in the 18th century and may well have much earlier origins. It starts near Plowden, which was a gathering point for drovers, and follows the spine of the Long Mynd towards Shrewsbury. It is a bridleway or BOAT for most of its length and crosses a fine stretch of heather moorland owned by the National Trust.

STAFFORDSHIRE

Prehistoric

South of Wetton, Stable Lane (SK117540) passes several bronze age burial mounds including the unique Long Low and the Bincliff Lead Mines.

SUFFOLK

The Environment and Transport Department sent me a very useful printout from the County Sites and Monuments Record (SMR) which includes eighteen listed 'hollow ways'. Some of these are included in the main body of the book, but here is the complete list.

TL 895- 573-, TM 2982 5156, TM 0793 7565, TM 222- 583-, TL 9100 7712, TL 623- 681-, TL 743- 655-, TL 7040 6670, TM 265- 598, TL 878- 481-, TL 890- 485-, TM 362- 898-, TM 213- 550-, TL 8254 8427, TM 0600 5760, TM 284- 372-, TL 9120 4355, TM 4885 8350.

SURREY

Roman

The line of the road known as Stane Street is today represented by a green lane in the area between Dorking and Ashstead. The best stretch is known as Pebble Lane, and between the following grid references it is scheduled as an ancient monument (TQ180540-195568).

EAST SUSSEX

Roman

The Chalvington and Ripe Field systems still survive well and include green lanes, some of which joined the two systems.

Drovers' routes

The County Planning Department undertook a pilot study in 1993, looking at a series of droveways between Bishopstone, an Archiepiscopal Manor, and Heathfield, its outlier in the High Weald. As is so often the case, financial constraints meant that the study was never broadened, nor was the work published anywhere.

The county has developed a methodology used in the study, which is reproduced on page 112.

WEST SUSSEX

Within their general publications list and the South Downs Way, many of the routes described contain green lanes.

WARWICKSHIRE

There are two RUPPs in the County, and work on some 280 claimed (but not confirmed) BOATs has barely begun. Similarly, a study into the County Highway Record is proposed for later in the year; subsequently there will be a review of the Unclassified County Road network and its interface with the Definitive Map.

As you can see from the above, specific studies on green lanes on a county basis have been few. To date the following have been surveyed: Cambridgeshire, Cornwall, Devon, Dorset (Dartington Institute Study), the High Peak (Dartington Institute Study), Lincolnshire and East Sussex.

ECOLOGY

The Fern Paradise

I am listing below a breakdown of ferns which you may find in green lanes as an illustration of the great wealth of wildlife which these lanes support. One could make just a detailed study of lichens or umbellifers, and easily fill a book.

The illustrations of ferns (below right) are taken from *The Fern Paradise* by Francis George Heath, published in 1908. One feels that the method of reproduction on photographic plates must have been a great luxury in this book. But ferns easily align themselves to luxury; they are the doyens of luxuriant growth. In order to identify the different types, it is only necessary to see how the leaves are shaped and how they are placed on the stem in relation to each other.

What is a fern? The simple diagram at the back of the colour plates should help. The main varieties are as follows: Single British ferns, Polypodies, Shield ferns, Spleenworts, Buckler ferns, Bladder ferns, Woodsias and Filmy ferns.

Although not so popular today, there was a time when indoor ferns were to be seen gracing many a Victorian parlour. Given the recent trend in limestone garden furniture, which is leading to over-quarrying in the UK, let us be thankful that ferns are being left to luxuriate in their natural habitat.

Descriptions of selected ferns

Firstly, bracken is not a fern. Bracken leaves spring from the stem of the plant and not the crown. The leaves do not grow diametrically opposed on the stem. Bracken is rough in texture and acquires a bronze tinge soon after it grows to its summer height. The invasiveness of its growth is well known to all landowners and gardeners.

The Polypodies

They are so called because the spore cases on the reverse of the leaves are not protected by a filmy covering. The Common polypody is not to be confused with hard fern as its colour is lighter and its texture softer.

Shield Ferns

So called because of the shield-shaped scale covers which protect the roundish heaps of seed cases borne on the backs of the fronds.

The Spleenworts

The common or popular name was given to this group of ferns on account of an ancient belief in their power, when used as medicine, of curing splenetic affections. They are primarily rock dwellers. Black maiden hair spleenwort grows 18" to 2 feet in height. The first pair of leaves seem to be separate from the rest. It is light green in appearance and purple underneath, and thrives in walls and on bridges.

The Buckler Ferns

These are named after the shield shaped scales covering the clusters of spore cases attached to the backs of the fronds. The Male Fern is found in woods, hedgerows, hillsides and by the water's edge. Its non-diametrically opposed leaves are 2-3 feet in height. The Broad buckler fern has a crisp curled appearance and a purpley stem, with diametrically opposed leaves. They are are shorter on the lower than the upper side of stem.

The Red Data List for Birds

Red Data Lists provide records of all endangered species of flora and fauna along with their habitats throughout the British Isles. Here are some details from the list for birds. Green Lanes run through all 24 habitats described in the listing, but as there is a greater density of lanes in some, these are the ones I have selected. The lanes themselves as a habitat are most closely akin to the

The Buckler Ferns

1. Male Fern. 2. Broad Buckler Fern.
3. Hay scented B.B. fern.
4. Prickly toothed Buckler fern.
5. Mountain Buckler fern.
6. Marsh Buckler fern.

Single British Ferns

1. Bracken. 2. Hart's tongue. 3. Lady's fern.
4. Hard fern. 5. Royal fern.
6. True Maidenhair. 7. Parsley Fern.
8. Bristle Fern. 9. Moonwort.
10. Adder's tongue. 11. Little Adder's tongue.

Oak

Ivy

Shield Fern

Honeysuckle

Hard Fern

Bluebell

Dog Rose

Green Alkanet

Bramble

Violet

Yarrow

Goats Beard

Pineapple
Mayweed

Speedwell

'Broad-leaved and mixed woods' habitat. Use this chart along with the Hedgerow Survey Form to record the bird life of a lane. Remember these listed below are endangered, so should you spot them please inform the RSPB.

Broad-leaved Mixed Woods, including Upland and Northern Areas
Honey Buzzard, Barn Owl, Firecrest, Fieldfare, Redwing, Brambling, Red Kite, Goshawk, Black Grouse.

Lowland Heath
Dartford Warbler, Woodlark, Nightjar.

Improved pastures
Grey Partridge, Corncrake, Barn Owl, Cirl Bunting, Red Kite, Montagu's Harrier, Marsh Harrier, Whimbrel, Chough, Redwing, Golden Plover, Hen Harrier.

Wet Lowland Grasslands
Spotted crake, ruff, black-tailed godwit, curlew, barn owl, Montagu's harrier, marsh harrier, golden plover, redshank, hen harrier.

Salt Marshes and Intertidal Flats
Wintering birds and passerines. Ringed Plover, Grey Plover, Black-Tailed Godwit, Curlew, Redshank, Knot, Dunlin, Sanderling.

Rivers and Streams
Tremmink's Stint, Marsh Warbler, Goldeneye, Osprey, Cetti's Warbler.

Plantations
Goshawk, Firecrest, Crested Tit, Nightjar, Woodlark, Hen Harrier, Goldeneye, Osprey, Merlin, Golden Oriole.

Arable Land
Grey Partridge, Stone Curlew, Cirl Bunting, Barn Owl, Montagu's Harrier, Marsh Harrier, Golden Plover, Teal, Hen Harrier.

Downland
Stone Curlew, Hen Harrier.

Appendix IV

SOME IMPORTANT EVENTS IN HIGHWAY HISTORY

History of highway maintenance

1140   Order of King Stephen: Lords of the Manor to keep highways open.

1285   King Edward I's Trench Act: roads through woods were to be 60 feet wide on either side of the King's Way.

1291   Papal Taxation list of parishes in England (see page 37).

1293   Statute of Winchester: all highways from one market town to another were to be enlarged so that there is no dyke or bush within 200 feet on either side (a bow shot).

1316   Nomina Villarum listed all English villages.

1334   The Lay Subsidy Rolls (For residents?)

1531   'C' stones were put up one hundred yards either side of a bridge.

1536   Bridges were to have parapets 3' or more in height, to deter robbers.

1555   Statute of Phillip and Mary: parishes to maintain roads. There was an elected surveyor and a system of voluntary labour, later amended in 1601.

1563   Elizabeth I: voluntary labour days increased from 4 to 6 per person.

1654   The Commonwealth: the Government was given powers to levy a local rate for the construction of roads.

1663   First turnpike (toll-paying road) introduced into this country.

1766-73 The General Turnpike Acts.

1835   The Highway Act: this established parish and district surveyors, highways boards and jurisdiction of Petty Sessions to levy fines.

1875   The Public Health Act: divided England into Urban and Rural Districts and created Urban Sanitary Districts.

1878   Highways and Locomotive (Amendment) Act Highways Authorities formed.

1889   County Councils took over both the responsibility for and the cost of main roads.

1894   Rural District Councils accepted responsibility for local roads.

1909   Central Government makes grants to local authorities for roads.

1920   Ministry of Transport first appears.

1930   County councils take over responsibility for all roads.

1936   Trunk roads become the responsibility of the MoT.

A record of highway maintenance

(After Tate's Parish Chest)

The Great Highway Act (1557)

Every parishioner for every ploughland in tillage or pasture that he occupied within the parish, and every person keeping a draught of horses or plough in the parish, had to provide for FOUR DAYS IN THE YEAR one wain, or cart furnished after the custom of the country . . . and also two able men with the same. Every other householder, cottager and labourer, able to labour and being no hired servant by the year, had either to put in four days' labour or to send 'one sufficient labourer' in his stead. This figure four was changed to six by Elizabethan legislation. The supervision of this 'statute labour' was entrusted to an unpaid surveyor of highways. His duties were:

1) Keeping accounts, fines and commutations and compositions.
2) Looking out for vehicles with too many horses.
3) Attending highway sessions in neighbouring towns.
4) Fixing on the dates for labour, the labourers and fining defaulters.
5) Pay a pound fine if he refused the position!

As it was unpopular, the surveyor's job was passed around in rotation or by house-row. Labourers often used to spend their six days begging. The surveyor carting materials used to mend the roads which ran through his own lands.

This legislation was incorporated in the 1601 Poor Law Act (and BTCV volunteers think themselves hard done by).

A methodology for research in green lanes

The following is a summary of the methodology used by East Sussex County Council in one of their studies of green lanes. This may be useful to any organization or individual wishing to make a similar study.

1. *Networking.* A list of useful contacts, both individual people and organizations.
2. *Library research and background reading.* See the Bibliography at the end of this book, and build up your own list of local publications.
3. *Definitive Rights Of Way maps.* The use of the Definitive Map provides a starting point for plotting roads that have been in use from time immemorial but are not "sealed against water" (i.e. tarmacked).
4. *Scanning aerial photographs.* Useful for recognizing footpaths without boundary hedges.
5. *County Sites and Monuments Record (SMR).* Search for roads, tracks, holloways and linear features.
6. *Map regression.* Compare the 6-inch OS maps with the 1:10,000 maps, which show the definitive ROWs. This process will eliminate any very modern tracks.
7. *Fieldwork and recording.* Having completed the above stages, choose a pilot area and begin site visits.

Appendix V

ARCHIVES FOR HISTORICAL RESEARCH

Archives at a National level
Website for Public Records Office: www.Hmc.gov.uk

Useful handbooks in the Public Records Office, Chancery Lane
Domesday Re-bound: Notes on the physical features and history of the
 Record (No.2, 1954).
The Records of the Forfeited Estates Commission (No. 12, 1968).
Chancery Records.
Lists of Plans annexed to Enclosure Awards, 31 Geo.11-7 William IV (App.
 D.K. Rep.26).
Exchequer Records.
Exchequer (T.R.) Ancient Deeds (AS and WS) (Lists and Indexes 158).
Exchequer, Treasury of the Receipt: Ancient Deeds Series A (L & I Soc. 151, 152).
Exchequer, Augmentation Office: Calendar of Ancient Deeds Series B (L & I
 Soc. 95, 101, 113, 124); and Ancient Deeds Series BB (E 328) (L & I Soc. 137).
State Papers and Modern Departmental Records.
Inland Revenue, Tithe Maps and Apportionments (IR 29, IR 30). This list is
 arranged by counties.
Ministry of Transport, Railway Dept. Papers (MT 6) (L & I Soc. 107, 114, 123).
Ironbridge Gorge Institute, Telford, Shropshire TF8 7AW. Tel 01952 432751,
 Fax 01952 432237. <www.ironbridge.org.uk>.
Public Records Office, Chancery Lane, WC2A ILR. Tel 0208 8763444.
Public Records Office, Ruskin Avenue, Kew, Richmond, Surrey TW9 4DU.
 Tel 0208 8763444.
The British Library Map Library, 96 Euston Road, London NWI 2DB. Tel 0207
 4127676. The national map library, with a collection of one and three quarter
 million atlases, maps, globes and books on cartography, dating from the fif-
 teenth century to the present day. **N.B. The following maps must be ordered
 a day in advance: Large-Scale Ordnance Survey National Grid maps of Great
 Britain (1:1250 or 50 inches to the mile) from the 1950s onwards.**
House of Commons Library, for the original Turnpike Acts. Tel 0207 219 3000.
The Kithead Trust (a national transport archive). In 1994 the Department of
 Transport decided that to retain their historical library was a luxury they
 could ill afford. The archive material dealing with road history was added
 to the existing Kithead collection. It can be consulted at De Salis Drive,
 Hampton Lovett, Droitwich Spa WR9 OQE. Tel 01905 776681.
Aerofilms Limited, Gate Studios, Station Road, Borehamwood WD6 IEJ. Tel
 0208 2070666.

PLACE NAMES

There are many books and papers which address the issue of names such as 'grendle' and 'grindle'. The names appears in books dealing with Celtic history and 'The Green Man'.

1. Associated with agriculture and industry
Assart (the process of deforestation which sometimes left green lanes behind).

Baulk Lane

Quarry Lane

Tanpits Lane

Lode Lane

Sandy Lane

2. Associated with droving
Booths

Butts Lane (where archery was practised)

Black Lane (as in Death, or maybe it was just dark)

Conney Lane (for rabbit poaching)

Doughy Lane (where the dusty miller lived)

Drift Lane

Droveden

Farthing

Gallows Gate, sometimes corrupted to Glazegate

Goosey

Jagger Lane (associated with pedlars and merchants)

Limers Gate

Lych Way

Lyke Wake

Marldon (Clay Lane)

Oxway

Penfold

Pinfold Halfpenny

Red Way (can refer to early red clay sites for pottery-making)

Rothern

Shieling

Turbury (Peat Paths)

3. Others
Rod (variation of road, mentioned 50 times in Anglo-Saxon charters)

Salters Lane

Saltersgate

Salterhebble

Street/stræt

weg (changing to way in modern English)

Wich

Silverhead Lane (often referring to the shiny nature of lane's surface)

Shuel Lane (shovel lane)

Slipperstone Lane, after the dangerous nature of the surface

Truss Ways (for the transportation of hay and grain harvests)

Place names connected with boundaries

Calenge	challenge, dispute	*Maere*	boundary, border.
Ceast	strife, contention.	*Mearc*	boundary
Crioch	a boundary (Scotland)	*Ra*	land-mark boundary
Devise	division, boundary (e.g.	*Ran*	boundary, strip or balk
	Viza, Vizacombe,	*Rima*	rim, edge, border
	Devon, Devizes)	*Scead*	separation
Ecg	edge	*Skial*	boundary
Flit	strife, dispute	*Taecels*	boundary mark or
Fyn	end, boundary		boundary
Gemaere hagan	boundary hedge	*Teo*	boundary
Grima	mark or blaze on a tree	*threap*	a dispute or contention
	to denote a boundary.		
Har	grey, hoary (hoarstone)	Most of these elements come from
Land-gemaere	land boundary	Anglo-saxon and have undergone
Land-scearu	landmark, boundary,	considerable pronunciation and
	share of land	spelling changes over the centuries.

Some of the commonest elements in English place names

bearu	(Old English)		wood (~barrow, ~beare, ~borough, ~bury)
burh		OE	fort, town (~brough, ~burgh, ~bury, ~borough,
			~burgh, ~bury, ~bourne, ~burn)
cot		OE	cottage, shed, shelter (~coate, ~cott)
denu		OE	valley (~dean)
haeg		OE	fence, enclosure (our modern hedge) (~hay, ~hey)
ham		OE	homestead, farm village (~ham)
maere		OE	boundary (~mar, ~mer, ~mere)
stow		OE	place of worship (~stow, ~stowe)
stret, stræt		OE	roman road (~street, ~strat, ~streat)
tun	OE		enclosure (~ton, ~tone)
wic	OE		group of buildings (~wich, ~week)
worth		OE	enclosure (~worth, ~worthy, ~wardine)

ORGANIZATIONS
& OTHER CONTACTS

'Discovering green lanes' website
There is a website from which you can download educational material:
<www.greenbooks.co.uk/greenlanes.htm>.

Organizations
All Wheel Drive Club, 19 Wildwood Glade, Hempstead, Gillingham, Kent ME7 3SX.

Amateur Motor Cycle Association, 28 Mill Park, Hawks Green Lane, Cannock, Staffordshire WS11 2XT.

ATB Landbase, National Agricultural Centre, Stoneleigh, Kenilworth, Warwickshire CV8 2RX. Tel 01203 696996.

Auto-Cycle Union, Wood Street, Rugby, Warwickshire. Tel 01788 540519.

The British Driving Society, 27 Dugard Place, Barford, Warwick CV35 8DX. Tel 01926 624420.

British Motorcyclists' Federation, 129 Seaforth Avenue, New Malden, Surrey KT3 6JU.

British Off Road Driving Association, "Westerings", Station Road, WEst Haddon, Northamptonshire, NN6 7AU.

BTCV, 36 St. Mary's Street, Wallingford, Oxford OX10 0EU. Tel 01491 821600. <information@btcv.org.uk> <www.btcv.org>.

BTCV Enterprises Ltd (Tools and Trading), Conservation Centre, Balby Road, Doncaster DN4 0RH. Tel 01302 859522.

The British Horse Society, Stoneleigh Deer Park, Kenilworth, Warwicks CV8 2XZ. Tel 01926 707700, Fax 01926 707800.
<enquiry@bhs.org.uk> <www. bhs.org.uk>.

Byways and Bridleways Trust, PO Box 117, Newcastle-upon-Tyne, NE3 5YT. Tel/Fax 0191 236 4086. <bbt@highwayman.demon.co.uk>. They produce a useful quarterly news-sheet with many instances of how legal cases have been contended.

Common Ground, Gold Hill House, 21 High Street, Shaftesbury, Dorset SP7 8JE.

Council for British Archaeology, Bowes Morrell House, 111, Walmgate, York, North Yorkshire, YO1 9WA. Tel 01904 671417, Fax 01904 671384. <archaeology@compuserve.com> <www.britarch.ac.uk>.

Council for the Protection of Rural England, Warwick House, 25, Buckingham Palace Road, London SW1W OPP. Tel 020 797 66373, Fax 020 797 66433. <info@cpre.org.uk> <www.greenchannel.com/cpre>.

Countryside Agency, John Dower House, Crescent Place, Cheltenham GL50 3RA. Tel 01242 521381 Fax 01242 584270. <enquiries@countryside.gov.uk> <www.countryside.gov.uk>.

Cycling Touring Club, 69 Meadrow, Godalming, Surrey GU7 3HS. Tel 01483 417217, Fax 01483 426994. <cycling@ctc.org.uk> <www.ctc.org.uk>.

Country Landowners' Association, 16 Belgrave Square, London SW1X 8PQ. Tel 020 7235 0511, Fax 020 7235 4696. <mail@cla.org.uk> <www.cla.org.uk>.

Department of the Environment, Transport and the Regions, Eland House, Bressenden Place, London SW1E 5DU. Tel 020 7944 3000. <www.detr.gov.uk>. A particularly useful publication is *A Practical Guide on Managing the Use of Vehicles on Public Rights of Way* (Feb 1998).

English Heritage, Fortress House, 23 Savile Row, London W1X 1AB. Tel 020 7973 300 Fax 020 7973 3435. <www.english-heritage.org.uk>.

English Nature, Northminster House, Peterborough, PE1 1UA. Tel 01733 455000, Fax 01733 56834. <enquiries@englishnature.org.uk>.

European Federation for Transport in the Environment, Rue de la Victoire 26, 1060 Brussels, Belgium. Fax (+ 32) 2 537 7394.

Forestry and Arboriculture Safety Training Council, 231 Corstorphine Road, Edinburgh EH12 7AT. Tel 01313 340303.

Farming and Wildlife Advisory Group (FWAG), The Lodge, Sandy, Bedfordshire SG19 2DL. Consult your local telephone directory.

GLEAM (Green Lanes Environmental Action Movement), PO Box 5206, Reading RG7 6YT. An unincorporated Association of individuals and groups whose aims are to ensure that unsurfaced highways carrying public rights of way (other than those already classified as footpaths or bridleways in accordance with the law) are preserved from damage caused by motorized vehicles of all kinds.

The Green Lane Association, SW contact: Mr. Steve Addicott, 35 Burcott Road, Wells, Somerset BA5 2EF.

Greenways The partners are regional governments in France and Belgium, the Grand Duchy of Luxembourg, Heritage Council in Ireland, the European Greenways Association and ourselves. Their quiet roads demonstration areas are in Norfolk, Kent and Devon, although there is interest from far wider afield. <Jacqui.Stearn@countryside.gov.uk> <Greenways@countryside.gov.uk>

The Long Distance Walkers Association c/o Brian Smith, 10 Temple Park Close, Leeds LS15 1JJ. Tel 01132 642205. <www.ldwa.org.uk>.

Milestones 2000 c/o Mervyn Benford, Cloudshill Cottage, High Street, Shutford, Banbury OX15 6PQ. Tel/Fax answerphone 01295 780308. A relatively new organization set up on a nationwide basis to record and preserve mileposts and stones, boundary stones and early finger posts in the UK.

Motoring Organizations' Land Access and Recreation Association (LARA), Tim Stevens, PO Box 20, Market Drayton, Shropshire TF9 1WR.

National Grid Tree Warden Scheme, 51 Catherine Place, London SW1E. Tel 020 7828 9928, Fax 020 7828 9060. <www.treecouncil.org.uk>.

The National Trust, 36 Queen Anne's Gate, London SW1H 9AS.

The Open Spaces Society, 25A Bell Street, Henley-on-Thames, Oxon RG9 2BA.

Ordnance Survey, Romsey Road, Southampton, SO16 4GU. Tel 01703 792000 or 08456 050505, Fax 0238 0792615. <enquiries@ordsvy.gov.uk> <www.ordsvy.gov.uk>.

The Ramblers Association, 2nd floor Camelford House, 87-90 Albert Embankment, London SE1 7TW. Tel 020 7339 8565, Fax 020 7339 8501. <enquiries@london.ramblers.org.uk> <www.ramblers.org.uk>.

The Rough Stuff Fellowship (for cyclists and mountain bikers). <www.rsf.org.uk>.

Royal Society for the Protection of Birds, The Lodge, Sandy, Beds, SG19 2DL. Tel 01767 680551, Fax 01767 692365. <bird@rspb.demon.co.uk>. <www.rspb.org.uk>.

Save our Hedges, 'Weekend' magazine, *The Daily Telegraph*, 1 Canada Square, Canary Wharf, London E14 5DT.

Sustrans, PO Box 21, Bristol BS99 2HA. Tel 0117 929 0888. <info@sustrans.org.uk> <www.sustrans.org.uk>.

The Trail Riders Fellowship, PO Box 196, Derby DE1 9EY.

The Woodland Trust, Autumn Park, Grantham, Lincolnshire NG31 6LL. Tel 01476 581111, Fax 01476 590808. <www.woodland-trust.org.uk>.

Appendix VIII
BIBLIOGRAPHY

Chapter 1

Hawkins, M.R.H., *Devon Roads*. Devon Books. 1988.

Hoskins, W.G., *The Making of the English Landscape*. 1955.

Schama, S., *Landscape and Memory*, HarperCollins, 1995.

Smiles, Samuel, *Lives of the Great Engineers* contains profiles of such road makers as Thomas Telford.

Chapter 2

Barnes, B., *Passage Through Time*. Saddleworth, 1981.

Belloc, Hilaire, *The Old Road*. 1910.

Belloc, Hilaire, *The Stane Street*. 1913.

Boyes, M. and Chester, H., *Great Walks: North York Moors*.

Blair, John, *Mediæval Surrey*. 1988.

Brandon, Peter, *The Sussex Countryside*. Hodder and Stoughton, 1974.

Cochrane, C., *The Lost Roads of Wessex*. Newton Abbot, 1969.

Cossons, *The Turnpike Roads of Nottinghamshire*. 1934.

Crosher, G.R., *Along the Cotswold Ways*.

Crummy, R.D., Hillam, J. and Crossan, C. 1982, 'Mersea Island: the Anglo-Saxon Causeway', *Essex Archaeology and History* 14, 77-86.

Dodd, A.E. and E. M., *Peakland Roads and Trackways*. Moorland Publishing, Ashbourne, 1974.

Down the Deep Lanes. Devon Books: Halsgrove Direct, Halsgrove House, Lower Moor Way, Tiverton, Devon EX16 6SS.

Dunn, M., *Walking Ancient Trackways*. 1986.

Fuller, G.J., 1953. *The Development of Roads in the Surrey Sussex Weald and Coastlands between 1700 and 1900*.

Groves, R., *Roads and Tracks in Gill's Dartmoor: A New Study*. Newton Abbot.

Harley, J.B., *Ordnance Survey Maps: A Descriptive Manual*. Southampton, Ordnance Survey, 1975.

Hemery, E., *Walking Dartmoor's Ancient Tracks*. 1986.

Hey, D., *Packmen, Carriers and Packhorse Roads; trade and communication in north Derbyshire and south Yorks*. Leicester University, Dept. of Communications, 1980.

Hinchcliffe, Ernest, *A Guide to the Packhorse Bridges of England*. Cicerone Press, Milnthorpe, LA7 7PY.

Hindle, B.P, 'Roads and Tracks' in L Cantor (ed), *The English Mediæval Landscape*, London, Croom Helm, 1982.

Hippisley Cox, R., *The Green Roads of England*. 1927.

Hodgkiss, A.G., *Discovering Antique Maps*. Shire Publications 1977.

Hooke, D., *The Reconstruction of Ancient Routeways*. The Local Historian, 1977.

Hurley, Heather, *The Old Roads of South Herefordshire*. Pound House, 1992.

Jones, B. & Mattingly D., *An Atlas of Roman Britain*. 1900.

Kanefsky, *Devon Tollhouses*. Exeter Industrial Archæology Group.

Lincolnshire County Council, *Green Lanes Project report*. September 1990.

Lowe, M., *The Turnpike Trusts in Devon and their Roads*. Transactions of the Devonshire Association, December 1990.

Luck, Liz, *Green Lane Walks in South-East Cornwall*. Liskeard, Breton Press. 1985.

Margary, I.D., *Roman Roads in Britain*. 1973.

Mingay, *Agricultural History of England from 1750-1850*. Volume 5 provided material for the Drovers and Packhorses chapter.

Peel, J.H.B., *Along the Green Roads of Britain*. 1976.

Roberts., *Translations of Stokenham Manorial Manor Rolls*.

Robinson, Bruce, *The Norfolk Walker's Handbook (A passing glance at our roadside heritage)*. Elmstead Publications, 1998.

Rutland County Council, *Turnpikes and Royal Mail of Rutland*. Spiegl Press, 6, Georges Street, Stamford, Lincs.

Stewart, Gerry., 'Tracks, ways and Roman roads' in *Grassroots* magazine. Gloucestershire C.C. 1993-1995.

Sullivan, D., *Ley Lines*. Wooden Books 1999.

Taylor, C., *Fields in the English Landscape*. Sutton, 1987.

Thomas, *Chronology of Devon's Bridges*. Transactions of the Devonshire Association, December 1992.

Toulson, S., *The Moors of the Southwest: Exploring the Ancient Tracks of Sedgemoor and Exmoor*.

Toulson, S., *The Moors of the Southwest 2: Exploring the Ancient Tracks of Dartmoor, Bodmin and Penwith*.

Toulson, S., *The Drovers*. Shire Publications, 1980.

Viatores, The: 1964. *Roman Roads of the South-East Midlands*.

Wright, G.N., *Turnpike Roads*. 1992.

Wright, G.N., *Roads and Trackways of the Yorkshire Dales*. Ashbourne. 1985.

Wright, G.N., *Roads and Trackways of Wessex*. Ashbourne. 1988.

Chapter 3

Albert, W., *The Turnpike Road System in England 1663-1840*. Cambridge. 1972.

Anderson, R.M.C., *The Roads of England*. 1932.

Belloc, Hilaire, *The Road* (Manchester). 1927.

Belsey, V.R., *Cornwall Roads Past and Present*. Silverlink, 1995.

Belsey, V.R., *Devon Roads Past and Present*. Past & Present Series, Silverlink, 1994.

Belsey, V.R., *The Green Lanes of England*. Green Books, 1998.

Beresford, M., *History on the Ground*. Sutton, 1957.

Bonser, K.J., *The Drovers*. 1970.

Brown and Fowler, *Early Land Allotment*. BAR, 1978.

Cameron, David Kerr, *The English Fair*. Sutton Publications 1998.

Chatwin, Bruce, *The Songlines*. Pan 1987.

Copeland, J., *Roads and their Traffic: 1750-1850*. Newton Abbot.

Crofts, J., *Packhorse, Waggon and Postland Carriage and Communications under the Tudors and Stuarts*. 1967.

Dawson, G.E. and Kennedy-Skipton, L., *Elizabethan Handwriting 1500-1650*. Faber 1968.

Friend, John B., *Cattle of the World*. Blandford Press: 1978.

Fiennes, C., *The Illustrated Journeys of Celia Fiennes*. Ed. C. Morris, 1982.

Finberg, *The Agrarian History of England and Wales*. Vols I and II, 1972.

Gooder, E.A., *Latin for Local History*. Longmans, reprinted 1970.

Gregory, J.W., *The Story of the Road*. 1931.

Hindle, B.P., *Maps for Local History*. 1988.

Hindle, B.P., *Mediæval Roads*. Shire Publications, 1989.

Hindle, B.P., *Mediæval Town Plans*. Shire Publications, 1990.

Hindle, B.P., *Roads, Tracks and their Interpretation*. 1993.

Humble, Richard., *The Fall of Saxon England*. Book Club Associates,1975.

Hindley, G., *A History of Roads*. 1971.

Hogg, *Inns and Villages of England*. Newnes, 1966.

Jackman, W.T., *The Development of Transportation in Modern England*. Cambridge, 1916.

Johnston, D.E., *Roman Roads in Britain*. Bourne End, 1979.

Jusserand, J.J., *English Wayfaring Life in the Middle Ages*. Fisher Unwin, 1889.

Pawson, E., *Transport and Economy: the Turnpike Roads of Eighteenth Century Britain*.

Rackham, O., *The History of the Countryside*, J.M. Dent, 1993.

Reader, W.J., *Macadam*.

Rowley, T., *Villages in the English Landscape*. 1987.

Ryecraft A. *Sixteenth and Seventeenth Century Handwriting* Series Borthwick Institute, York, 3rd rev. edn. 1972.

Sawyer, P.H. *Anglo-Saxon Charters: an annotated list and bibliography*, Royal Historical Society, London, 1968.

Scott, Giles C.W., *The Road Goes On*. 1946.

Semlyen, Anna, *Cutting Your Car Use*. Green Books 1998.

Sheldon, G., *From Trackway to Turnpike* (East Devon). 1928.

Stenton, *Anglo-Saxon England*. Oxford, 1971.

Stephens, W.B., *Sources for English Local History*, Phillimore. Revised ed. 1994.

Strong, L.A.G., *The Rolling Road*. 1956.

Tate W. E., *The Parish Chest*. Cambridge UP, 1969.

Taylor, C., *Roads and Tracks of Britain*. Sutton, 1979.

Thomas, J.M., *Roads before the Railways, 1700-1851*. 1970.

Turner, M., *English Parliamentary Enclosure*. 1980.

Watkins, A., *The Old Straight Track*. 1925.

Williamson, Henry, *The Lone Swallows*. Faber 1922.

Chapter 4

Aichele D. & R., Schwegler H. W. & A., *Wild Flowers of Britain & Europe.* Hamlyn, 1992.

Andrews, J., Rabane, M., *Farming and Wildlife: A Practical Management Handbook,* RSPB, 1994.

Arnold E.N., Burton J.A. & Overenden D.W., *A Field Guide to the Reptiles and Amphibians of Britain & Europe.* Collins, 1978.

Bellamy, David, *Discovering the Countryside with David Bellamy: Grassland Walks.* Newnes Books, 1983.

Blamey, Marjorie & Fitter, Richard, *Wild Flowers of Britain & Northern Europe.* Diamond Books, 1994.

British Trust for Conservation Volunteers, *Hedging,* 1987.

Burton, John A., *Field Guide to the Mammals of Britain & Europe.* Kingfisher Books, 1991.

Cummins, R et al. *Diversity in British Hedgerows* (Research Report for the Department of the Environment), Institute of terrestrial Ecology, Banchory, 1992.

Dowdeswell, W.H., *Hedgerows and Verges*, Allen and Unwin, 1987.

Evens, J. 1993 Hedgerow Management. Irish Organic Farmers and Growers Association.

Fitter, R. & A., and Farrer, Ann, *Collins Guide to the Grasses, Sedges, Rushes & Ferns of Britain & Northern Europe.* Collins, 1983.

Hart, E., *Hedgelaying and Fencing: the Countryman's art explained*, Thorsons 1981.

The Hedgerow Regulations: Your Questions Answered. A leaflet produced by the Department of the Environment, May 1997.

Heinsel, H., Fitter, R. & Parslow, J., *The Birds of Britain & Europe.* Collins, 1972.

Henderson, Robert K., *The Neighborhood Forager.* Chelsea Green Publishing Co, White River Junction, Vermont (distributed in the UK by Green Books).

Hodge, S.J. 1990. The Establishments of Trees in Hedgerows. Research Information. Note 195. Forestry Commission.

Hubbard, C.E., *Grasses.* Third edition. Penguin, 1984.

Lickorish, Su, *Wildflowers Work.* Landlife, National Wildflower Centre, 1997.

Mabey, R., *The Roadside Wildlife Book.* David and Charles, 1974.

Mabey R., *The Roadside Verge Book*, David and Charles.

Maclean, M., *New Hedges for the Countryside*, Farming Press 1992.

Marren, *A Regional Guide to Britain's Ancient Woodland*, English Nature.

Mitchell, Alan, *A Field Guide to the Trees of Britain & Northern Europe.* Collins, 1988.

Muir, R.N., *Hedgerows: Their History and Wildlife*, Michael Joseph, 1989.

Muir, R.N. *Fields,* Michael Joseph, 1989.

Muir, R. & Muir, N., *Hedgerows: Their History and Wildlife,* Michael Joseph, 1987.

Nature Conservancy Council and RSPB, *Red Data Birds in Britain*. Poyser 1990.

Pollard, E., Hooper, M.D. & Moore, N., *Hedges*, Collins 1974.

Phillips, Roger, *Native & Common Trees*. Elm Tree Books, 1986.

Stastny, Karel, *Birds of Britain & Europe*. Hamlyn, 1990.

Sterry, Paul, *Fungi of Britain & Northern Europe*. Hamlyn, 1991.

Silsoe College, *The Economics of Sustainable Hedge Cutting*, Silsoe College, 1995.

Thomas, E. & White, J.T., *Hedgerow*. Dorling Kindersley, 1982.

Verner, Yvette, *Creating a Flower Meadow*. Green Books 1998.

Watt, T.A. & Buckley, G.P. (eds.), *Hedgerow Management and Nature Conservation*, Wye College Press 1995.

Williamson, Henry, *The Lone Swallows*. Faber 1922.

Wilkinson, J. & Tweedie, M., *A Handguide to the Butterflies and Moths of Britain and Europe*. Treasure Press, 1986.

Wilson, *Hedgerows*. David and Charles.

Wilson, R., *The Hedgerow Book*, David and Charles, 1979.

Zahradnik, J. & Severa, F., *The Illustrated Book of Insects*. Treasure Press, 1991.

Chapter 5

Countryside Commission Pamphlet No. 186, *Out in the Country*.

Dartington Institute Study on Green Lanes 1976.

Department of the Environment, Transport and the Regions, *Making the Best of Byways*, a practical guide on managing the use of vehicles on Public Rights of Way.

Drake, J., *The Motorways*. 1969.

Dyos, H.J., and Aldcroft, D.H., *British Transport: An Economic Survey from the Seventeenth Century to the 20th*. Leicester University Press, 1969.

A Guide to Definitive Map Procedures, The Countryside Commission, January 1998.

Pick, C., *Off the Motorway*. Cadogan and Century Books.

Rights of Way—A Guide to law and practice by John Ridall and John Trevelyan, copublished by the Open Spaces Society and the Ramblers Association (ISBN: 0-900613 -73-4).

'Rights of Way' CD-ROM. Produced by the Countryside Agency, The Institute of Public Rights of Way Officers, the County Surveyors Society, The Local Government Association. Copies available from George Keeping <editor@prowgpg.org>. £15 by post (PROW GPG, Box 6502, Sleaford, Lincolnshire NG34 7WU).

Webb, Sidney & Beatrice, *English Local Government, The Story of the King's Highway*. 1913.

Zuckermann, Wolfgang., *End of the Road, The World Car Crisis and How We Can Solve It*. Chelsea Green, White River Junction, 1991.

INDEX

Main entries for a particular
subject are in bold

Also available:

THE GREEN LANES OF ENGLAND

Valerie Belsey

"I salute Valerie Belsey as a tenacious champion of green lanes. The strength of her book is that it will provoke understanding, and nurture care, for this precious part of England's heritage."—from the Foreword by Michael Dower

We value green lanes for recreational use, yet they also have great cultural and historical value: their contours, surfaces and routes reflect the goods and people that used them through the centuries, whether pilgrims, packhorses or cattle drovers. *The Green Lanes of England* explores the history and present state of our remaining network of green lanes, on a local and national basis, and the opinions of conflicting user groups and county councils are also discussed. *The Green Lanes of England* will provide a new tool for understanding how to read the English landscape, which has been and continues to be moulded by the roads which pass through it.

Green Books 160pp with 70 colour and 70 b&w photos, maps, line drawings, appendices, bibliography and index 216 x 197mm ISBN 1 870098 69 2 £12.95 pb

Order through your local bookshop, or direct from the publishers:

Green Books, Foxhole, Dartington,
Totnes, Devon TQ9 6EB
Tel: 01803 863260 Fax: 01803 863843
sales@greenbooks.co.uk
www.greenbooks.co.uk

Also available:

CREATING
A FLOWER MEADOW

Yvette Verner

"This is an inspiring story of our times . . . but it is much more than that, for it is a vade mecum of how it was done and how you—yes you, the reader—can do it for yourself."—from the Foreword by David Bellamy

Inspired by the idea of doing something positive for their local environment, Yvette Verner and her husband Mike bought a small field close to their home in the south of England. With the bountiful assistance of nature they created a flower meadow which attracts a rich variety of wildlife, including badgers, deer and a multitude of birds and butterflies.

Shows how you can create a natural habitat in your own garden, whether large or small, so you too can observe the lifestyles of our native flora and fauna, and play your part in encouraging their survival. Includes lists of species of flowers, grasses, trees, birds and butterflies, a seasonal calendar and contact addresses for further info.

**Green Earth Books 144pp with 40 line drawings and 16pp of
colour plates, bibliography and index 234 x 156mm
ISBN 1 900322 08 0 £9.95 pb**

Order through your local bookshop, or direct from the publishers:

Green Books, Foxhole, Dartington,
Totnes, Devon TQ9 6EB
Tel: 01803 863260 Fax: 01803 863843
sales@greenbooks.co.uk
www.greenbooks.co.uk